THE EVOLUTION OF MUSICAL FORM

This book is based on six lectures on the history of instrumental forms given by the author at the request of The Council of the Ferens Fine Arts Lectures, Hull University College, and their kind permission to use them is hereby acknowledged.

THE EVOLUTION OF MUSICAL FORM

by

EDWARD C. BAIRSTOW

Professor of Music in the University of Durham
Organist and Master of the Choir at York Minster

NEW YORK
COOPER SQUARE PUBLISHERS, INC.
1972

FOREWORD

THIS little book originated in six lectures delivered at University College, Hull, as the Ferens Lectures for 1940. The Ferens Lectures on art are given annually. They become the property of the Ferens Council, and are usually published by them. As local printing and publishing is difficult in war-time, Mr. J. H. Nicholson, the Principal of University College, suggested that the lectures should be submitted to the Oxford University Press, who kindly undertook to publish them in the form of a book.

My grateful thanks go to Mr. Nicholson and the Ferens Council for allowing me to use them in this way, and to the Oxford University Press for undertaking the work at a very difficult time.

When delivered at Hull, the time for each lecture was limited. Thus the illustrations were necessarily few, and had to be chosen so as to employ the artists available, supplemented with a few gramophone records. Many more examples of music have now been included, but the book is still designed for the same type of people as constituted the original audiences, namely, enthusiastic amateurs and young students, together with a sprinkling of professional musicians. Therefore examples have been chosen where possible from well-known works, likely to be in the library of the majority of readers. This obviates the trouble and expense of buying music. Moreover, pre-knowledge makes analysis much easier.

Technicalities have been avoided where possible, and the subject of Form, which has very little appeal for many musical people, because it is considered to be dull and academic, has perhaps been approached from a more human and friendly point of view than is to be found in the average text-book.

1942

ACKNOWLEDGEMENTS

Permission to reproduce certain music examples is gratefully acknowledged to the copyright owners:

Miss Maud Karpeles and Messrs. Novello and Co. Ltd. for: 'High Germany', 'A Farmer's Son so Sweet', 'Bruton Town', 'The Bold Fisherman', 'Green Bushes', from the Cecil Sharp Collection.

Dr. R. Vaughan Williams and Messrs. Novello and Co. Ltd. for: 'Bushes and Briars'.

Messrs. Stainer and Bell Ltd. for: 'The London Symphony', R. Vaughan Williams.

The Exors. of Baring-Gould and Messrs. Methuen and Co. Ltd. for: 'Matthew, Mark, Luke and John', from 'Songs of the West'.

Mrs. Graves for: 'The Sheep Under the Snow', from 'The Celtic Song Book'.

British and Continental Music Agencies, Ltd., for: Symphony No. 2, Sibelius.

CONTENTS

I

THE CADENCE

AN ability to recognize both by ear and by eye the different types of cadence is essential to the study of form, for cadences are music's means of punctuation. They mark the close of the phrases or sentences as well as the divisions of the form.

The word cadence (Latin *cadere*, to fall) was originally applied to the fall of the voice at the close of a sentence. And, as the earliest melodies followed the rise and fall of the voice in speech, they also ended with a fall, generally a drop of one note to what is now called the keynote or tonic, but which was then termed the final of the mode.

Shakespeare in *Twelfth Night* makes the Duke say:

> That strain again: it had a dying fall;
> O, it came o'er my ear like the sweet south,
> That breathes upon a bank of violets,
> Stealing and giving odour.

From these lovely lines we see that Shakespeare knew the technical name for a cadence, or fall, or close, and had also experienced its emotional effect.

Here is a melody in which every phrase except the second ends by the fall of one note. It is the traditional tune to the hymn, *Aeterna Christi Munera*, from *Directorium Chori* by Guidetti, 1582, a tune which so commended itself to Palestrina that he wrote a mass upon it.

1

The earliest attempt to harmonize this falling close was to

9

make another part sing the third below the penultimate note and then rise to join the other on the final, like this:

As the tune was often in the tenor part (Latin, *tenere*, to hold) the cadence was often inverted:

This rudimentary cadence is to be found as early as the year 1300.[1]

All music was originally entirely melodic. Naturally the first attempts to add a descant to a melody were only in two parts. The gradual increase in the number of parts meant additional notes in the cadence. Here is one for four parts:

Tune in Tenor

The next important step from our point of view was the introduction of the suspension. This might easily have been due to an error, for if some singer was late with the penultimate note of a cadence, a suspension would follow:

---

[1] See *Oxford History of Music*, Vol. i, pp. 239–40.

The beautiful effect of this would surely commend itself to the *Maestro di Capella*, or whoever was in charge. At all events it was incorporated in official counterpoint and is found as early as the middle of the fourteenth century.[1]

It was more than a hundred years later that the perfect cadence reached its present form. In the early years of the fifteenth century it is to be found in the works of Guilielmus Dufay[2] (b. before 1400, d. 1474) and his contemporaries of the first Netherland school, not as an occasional experiment or an accident, but as the regular and accepted means of bringing to a close each section of the music. By this time the ornamental resolution of the suspension by means of a little twiddle had made its appearance. This will be recognized by every one. It has been constantly used ever since:

The 'passing note' also was now common enough. Passing notes filled in the gaps between the harmony notes—those belonging to the particular chords employed at the moment —and moved in scale form up or down. They, like suspensions, may have been due to the vagaries of the singers. Even now they sometimes creep in. For instance, in Mendelssohn's tune to 'Hark the herald angels sing', one often hears:

Whereas Mendelssohn 7(a)
            wrote:

Composers now became aware that the notes added to the first primitive two-part close form the chord of the 'dominant' (the technical name for the fifth note of the scale, or mode) next in importance to the 'tonic' chord (tonic being the tech-

---

[1] See *Oxford History of Music*, Vol. i, p. 250.
[2] *Ibid.*, Vol. ii, p. 53, bar 1.

nical name for the keynote). They found that to place these chords in juxtaposition, dominant first, not only establishes the key from which these chords were drawn, but brings the music to a very definite full stop:

8

It naturally followed that any two chords very closely related to one another would have a similar effect. The root, or bass note of the dominant chord, lies a fifth above the keynote or tonic. It was soon evident that a cadence could be made with the chord whose root lies a fifth below, instead of a fifth above, the tonic. Then came into being the 'plagal', or ecclesiastical cadence—subdominant followed by tonic:

9

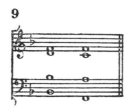

The common chord (a note sounded together with the major or minor third and perfect fifth above it) and its first inversion (when the bass, or lowest part has the third instead of the root), passing notes, and suspensions formed the entire vocabulary of composers from the period of Dufay to the beginning of the seventeenth century. Here is the last phrase of *Aeterna Christi* fully decked out with these adornments:

10

Two other types of cadence must be explained before the end of the purely technical part of this chapter is reached. The first is the comma or semicolon of music—the imperfect or half-cadence. This is made by bringing the phrase or section of the piece to a conclusion on the dominant chord. It is often preceded by the tonic, thus reversing the order of the chords in the perfect cadence:

But the effect of a half-close or comma can be obtained by preceding the dominant chord by one which has as its root any of the other notes of the scale:

One point must be noted here: there will be no effect of a close or partial close unless rhythm and harmony go hand in hand. The final chord must be reached on an accented beat of the bar, usually the first beat.

Composers have loved decoration for the last four hundred years, and two of the most popular devices have been the suspensions already explained, with their ornamental resolutions, and, very much later in musical history, upwards of two hundred years ago, the appoggiatura. This was the device of allowing any part in the harmony to proceed to a note lying next above or next below one of the notes of the chord and then to move on to the chord note:

Appoggiaturas were first written in small type to show that they were only a decorative and not a constructional element. Written thus, their length was often indefinite. Nowadays they appear in the same type as other notes. Very often at a cadence, although the bass would move from dominant to tonic at the end of a phrase, and although the final chord would appear on the accented beat, one or more of the other parts would be delayed by means of the decorative devices just referred to, and would come to rest at a later point than the bass, thus:

This delayed and decorated form of the cadence is often termed the 'feminine', whilst the plain, straightforward put-that-in-your-pipe-and-smoke-it type is known as the 'masculine' cadence. Many examples can be found in German Lieder, for German poetry has many lines ending in unaccented syllables. For instance, in Schubert's cycle, *Die Schöne Müllerin*, the third song 'Halt!' has eight feminine endings, and the sixth 'Der Neugierige' still more.

Finally, there is the interrupted or false cadence. This occurs when the dominant chord, as the first chord in a cadence, is not followed by the tonic as every one expects, but by some other more or less surprising harmony. This is useful for two purposes: first, when the melody notes suggest a perfect cadence but the end of the sentence is not reached, as for instance, in the twentieth bar of Beethoven's Piano Sonata in E minor, op. 90, and second, when the composer desires to shake up his audience for something exciting which follows immediately, as in Bach's Toccata in F for organ, Novello edition, Book IX, page 181, line 4, bar 5, or the sixth and seventh of the last thirteen bars of the first movement of Beethoven's Piano Sonata in F minor, op. 2, no. 1.

The hymn-tune, 'St. Peter' (E.H. 265, A. & M. 13), contains all the cadences except the plagal. If you append an Amen you get all four. The perfect cadence at the end of the first line firmly establishes the key. Then follows an imperfect or half-close to mark half-way house, then an interrupted cadence, where the melody has two notes concluding the third phrase which suggest a perfect cadence, though the end is not yet reached, and finally the perfect cadence.

Probably all four cadences can now be recognized. If there is any difficulty in differentiating between perfect and plagal, it should be remembered that the perfect always has one part falling to the keynote and a leading note going upwards to it, whilst in the plagal the keynote is present in both chords.

A series of beautiful examples of these cadences will now be considered; they will be taken in chronological order, beginning at the period when music emerged from its primitive stage and became palatable to modern ears—the period of the sixteenth century. But before doing so some conclusion must be reached as to the points of interest to be observed.

The first point is the fact that these four cadences have done duty as music's marks of punctuation for so long. It is only within the last fifty years or so that any attempt has been made to bring a composition to a close without either a perfect or a plagal cadence.

The next point is the way they have attracted composers. Some were evidently so much moved by their effect that they included one every few bars, and continually brought the music to a standstill, as in a hymn-tune. There is a little anthem by Adrian Batten (organist of St. Paul's Cathedral, d. 1637) which although only sixteen bars in length has ten cadences! (O.U.P. *Tudor Church Music*, No. 56.) This defect was often overcome by using the basic harmony of a cadence but allowing some part or parts to keep moving, and thus bridging over what would otherwise have been a complete stop.

The third point to notice is this: composers may be roughly divided into two classes, those who take things as they find them and leave it at that, and those who endeavour to impart variety and novelty by developing the ideas and enlarging the conventions of their predecessors. It has been said that when an art is flourishing healthily it invariably shows variety, the result of imagination and invention. This is indeed true, although in music there seem at first sight to be exceptions amongst the great masters. Bach and Mozart, for instance, used harmonic and contrapuntal idioms that were common in their time. They invented no new chords. They accepted the theories of their era, but they used them in a new way. Just as a man can speak or write beautiful English and can produce new and entrancing ideas though using only simple words that are in common use, so a great musician can take the materials he finds his contemporaries using to weave new patterns and express new thoughts. The other class of composers loves to experiment, to step out into the unknown, to invent. It will be interesting to see how both these types have used the cadence.

Let us begin with Palestrina and the sixteenth-century school. In their day the ancient ecclesiastical modes still existed and took the place of our major and minor scales. The modes originally included only the sounds which can be made without the use of sharps and flats: scales made entirely with the white notes of the piano, as we should put it. Now by experimenting it will be found that there are only two such scales which finish their ascending course with a semitone between the seventh and eighth notes. It will be remembered that the seed from which the perfect cadence grew was the fall of one note in the melody to the keynote, and the rise by a semitone of another part through what we call the leading note to the keynote. This was impossible in four of the modes—those beginning on D, E, G, and A—unless sharps were used. In three of them sharps did actually appear at all the perfect cadences, but in the other this was impossible, for in those days instruments were tuned to, and singers no doubt used, the unequally tempered scale—the natural scale, and this had no D sharp. And so the Phrygian mode—E to E—had its own cadence, the chord of D minor followed by the chord of E major. This is still known as the Phrygian cadence. This mode kept its peculiar atmosphere when the others, by the addition of sharps and flats, had become very much like major and minor scales. Here is a beautiful example of the mode and its cadence—the conclusion of Palestrina's motet, *Super flumina Babylonis*:

It will be noticed that at the third bar (marked by a square bracket) the music sounds as if it were about to stop at a perfect cadence on A. But at this moment the basses enter with the little tune marked by slurs. This makes an interrupted cadence and keeps the music moving on. Very often when the end of a sentence in the text demanded a cadence, Palestrina and his contemporaries[1] would avoid a lame halt by making a voice enter with the new sentence before the other voices had completed the cadence of the previous one, or so soon after that no sense of a stop is noticed.

Even in the sixteenth century, when only the suspensions and passing notes already mentioned were available as means of decoration, and when the only chords in use were the major and minor common chords and their first inversions (where the bass sings the third of the chord), wonderful lingering closes were written:

> In notes with many a winding bout
> Of linkèd sweetness long drawn out.

[1] Dufay knew how to do this. Refer again to the example quoted in the *Oxford History of Music*, Vol. ii, p. 53, and paragraph 1, p. 55.

Here are a few English examples:

16
The conclusion of the Anthem 'Hear the voice and prayer'

TALLIS (1520-85)

17
The final cadence of the Anthem 'O Lord, the Maker of all thing'

W. MUNDY (1530-91)

18
The conclusion of the Motet, *Ave verum*.

BYRD (1538-1623)

Our own composers of the Tudor period were inveterate experimentalists. They were no longer under the thumb of the Church as Palestrina and the Italians were. They invented a form of cadence sometimes called the 'English cadence'. Certainly it has been specially attractive to English composers right down to our own day. It was so common in the time of Good Queen Bess that Thomas Morley, our earliest theorist, condemns it. He says in his quaint dialogue between master and pupil:[1]

Master. For though the song were of ten or more parts yet would that point serve for one, not troubling any of the rest, but nowe a daies it is growne in such common use as

[1] *A plaine and easy introduction to practicall music*, by Thomas Morley, published 1597.

divers will make no scruple to use it in fewe partes where as
it might well enough be left out, though it be very usual
with our organists.

Polymathes [the pupil]. That is verie true, for if you wil
but once walke to Paules church, you shall here it three or
foure times at the least in one service if not in one verse.

The essential features of this cadence are (1) a suspension of
the tonic over the leading note, which immediately returns to
the tonic; (2) notes of the descending scale, particularly the
seventh, sixth, and fifth, heard simultaneously with the suspension, thus:

19

Sometimes the sharpened and flattened leading notes are heard
simultaneously, making a dissonance quite pungent even to
our modern ears.

20

From a motet, *In manus tuas*. TALLIS

Here follow a few examples of its use in later times. The
first, a specially beautiful example, is from Purcell's anthem,
'Remember not, Lord, our offences'. The English cadence is
marked with a square bracket. In this case it is used as an
interrupted cadence. The final cadence is also very lovely. It
has a double suspension and a dominant seventh.

21

The second example is from an anthem, 'Hear my crying' by Weldon (1676–1736), Purcell's pupil. He was so fond of the effect that he made each voice as it entered reproduce it.

22

The third is by Battishill (1738–1801). This is interesting because the words of the anthem ('O Lord, look down from heaven') finish with a query—'Thy mercies towards me, are they restrained?' And Battishill finishes not with a perfect cadence, but with a half-cadence on the dominant. In fact the whole anthem (and especially its conclusion) is remarkable for its modernity. It was written at an ultraconventional and generally uninspired period of English music.

23

The fourth is from S. S. Wesley's *Magnificat* in E, written in 1844. He, like Weldon, repeats the cadence several times as if he were loath to leave it.

24

Finally, there is an example from Dr. Harold Darke's *Credo* in F, published in 1926.

6

25

In the seventeenth century the anticipatory note made its appearance. The seventh note of the scale pressed forward eagerly to the eighth, or the second fell to the first, before the other parts moved from the penultimate chord of the cadence:

26

Purcell delighted to give this anticipatory note weight and length, thus giving greater pungency to the progression. Many modern editors fail to appreciate this. In fact in his well-known song, 'I attempt from love's sickness to fly', nearly every edition except that of the Purcell Society gives:

27

thou   canst   not   raise   for-ces   e - nough   to re - bel.

27(a)   **Whereas Purcell wrote:**

The harmonies are filled in from Purcell's figured bass, the sole accompaniment given by him.

Even in the decadent time which followed Purcell, English composers continued to use his bold dissonances, but in a timid and half-hearted way. One of their devices, frequently used, was to leave the dominant, which now often had a seventh imposed upon it:

28

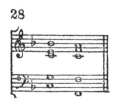

and proceed to another seventh on the bass note beneath it—
the subdominant—thus making consecutive discords. No
doubt this came into music through a type of cadence that was
common, namely dominant, subdominant, dominant, tonic, the
only difference being the seventh added to the subdominant
chord. This probably originated as a passing note, as in the
example:

29

The following cadence, from an anthem, 'I will arise and go
to my father' by Creyghton (1639–1733), shows its normal
form:

30

Perhaps this cadence led to a more modern type in which the
dominant and subdominant chords were combined, a mixture
of the perfect and plagal cadences, as for instance, the conclusion of the slow movement of Beethoven's Piano Sonata in D,
op. 10, no. 3.

Handel took the cadence with the long anticipatory note
from Purcell and used it often, as in this Aria, 'V'adoro,
pupille' from *Julius Caesar*:

31

He was the greatest of all masters in one respect—he could work marvels with the most simple and slender material. The thrilling opening of the Hallelujah Chorus from *Messiah* has no other harmonies than the three cadential chords: tonic, dominant, and subdominant. As a rule his cadences are very conventional. The formula he used most frequently is this, with two anticipatory notes:

When Robert Franz re-wrote Mozart's additional orchestral accompaniments to *Messiah* and added some of his own, he put an extra note into one of these chords practically every time this cadence appears:

This gave the cadence a most un-Handelian flavour, and showed that Franz was not very closely acquainted with the master's harmonic idiom. The military bands, by the way, did the very same thing when playing the 'Dead March' at the late King George V's funeral. This is quoted to show how keenly one must listen to music if all its secrets are to be revealed. To many people there is no difference between the real Handel and the false.

Purcell, Handel, and Bach used a little trick at some of their cadences which is rather interesting. They lived in a conventional age. One of the laws of the Medes and Persians was that the number of beats in a bar must not be varied in the same movement. The Elizabethans treated bar-lengths very freely, and thereby gave an elasticity to their rhythm which was lost in later times. These composers evaded the convention by writing three bars of duple time and putting them into two bars of triple, thus:

34   from *'Israel in Egypt',* Handel

Which thy hands have es - tab - lish- ed.

The amazing thing is that many singers, and even editors, have never realized this, and, thinking that Handel's verbal stresses were wrong, as they would be in triple time, have altered the words to make them fit a triple rhythm.

Bach also was often conventional in his cadences, though he wrote many of singular beauty. He loved to lengthen out both the dominant and tonic portions of a cadence by means of what are known as 'pedal points'. These no doubt originated from the fact that the first organ pedals were clumsy and heavy to play. When an organist got his foot on to one of them he was quite glad to keep it there. The discovery was then made that the dominant and tonic sounded quite well as bass notes even when the harmonies above them had no relationship with them, provided the first and last chords above them were dominant or tonic. The *Well-tempered Clavier,* or as it is better known, the Forty-eight Preludes and Fugues provide many splendid examples, for instance the first Prelude and Fugue, the fourth Fugue, the seventh Prelude, the twelfth Prelude, the twentieth Fugue, the twenty-fourth Fugue, all in Book I; the sixteenth and nineteenth Preludes, and the tenth and fifteenth Fugues from Book II.

After Bach and Handel's time, at the close of the eighteenth and the opening of the nineteenth centuries, two important developments occurred. One was the birth of sonata form, and the other the improvement in orchestral playing. Instead of the short, contrapuntal themes of the previous era, whole melodies were used as themes, and instead of one rhythmic figure prevailing throughout a whole movement, it was found that great effects could be obtained from contrasting one rhythmic figure with another. This idea was so novel and absorbing that composers found that for a while they could hold their audiences with nothing else. And so harmony and colour were neglected in favour of new rhythmic devices and the development of form. Moreover, the horns and trumpets of those days could play little more than the notes of the tonic chord, for they had no valves to give them the chromatic scale. Their only means of varying the pitch was by crooks, or curved tubes which fitted on to the instrument and by lengthening it flattened, or by shortening it sharpened, the pitch. This did not encourage composers to use harmonies containing notes which these instruments could not play. Whole movements were written with very little more than the three chords which made the cadences—tonic, dominant, and subdominant, and their derivatives. The works of Haydn, Mozart, and Beethoven contain so many examples that it is almost superfluous to quote any particular movement. The Minuet from Beethoven's Piano Sonata in E flat, op. 7, and the song, 'Deh vieni all finestra', from Mozart's *Don Giovanni*, are possibly as well known to the average reader as any others.

The reiteration of the cadence at the end of many compositions of this period, as in Beethoven's Fifth Symphony, seems needless to us nowadays. Presumably this apparently vain repetition was the result of two feelings: the joy that the composer must have felt on the completion of so wonderful a work, and the reluctance he had in leaving it. We have experienced the same feelings ourselves when finishing after a lengthy period some work which has cost us much, but has been a source of great pleasure. It might be said, why did not Beethoven think of something less cheap and ordinary? But it must be remembered that there was far more reverence for convention even in Beethoven's time than there is to-day, and that the conventional perfect and plagal cadences were the only means of finishing a piece of music then, and for many years afterwards.

Quite early in the seventeenth century, when the modern major and minor scales had supplanted the ecclesiastical modes, it was discovered that to alter a note in a chord chromatically, that is, to flatten or sharpen it by a semitone, often gave it a different and a richer colour. To go back to the first simple cadence of a sixth followed by an eighth (Ex. 3), the effect would now be:

35

Or, with the third added:

This was used as an imperfect or half-close even in those days. But changes in music moved very slowly until this century, so that it was not until the latter half of the nineteenth century that composers began to experiment with the hoary old cadences by sharpening or flattening other notes in the dominant or subdominant chords. Here are some of the results:

36

The dominant seventh (Ex. 28) was used even at the end of the sixteenth century, but it was many years before other notes were added to this chord. When they were it was fairly logical that they should be at the distance of a third above each other, as are the notes of a common chord or triad. Dissonance came into music very gradually: the interval of a third produced less than a second or fourth would have done. Here are cadences with the ninth, eleventh, and thirteenth (play Ex. 28 first):

37

When the chromatically altered notes were used along with the added notes many chords of different shades of colour were produced. The only stipulation was that enough should be left of the original chord to make the progression recognizable as a cadence. Here are a very few of the many combinations which resulted:

38

These only alter the first chord of the cadence. The final tonic chord has also had a note added to it very frequently, namely the sixth above the root:

39

II

PROVIDED we come into the world as healthy, normal babies, what we eventually become depends very largely on our habits, our associations, our thoughts. These affect our bodies as well as our minds. Probably no one is entirely unmoved by beauty of bodily shape in some form or another; either in a human being, an animal, or a bird. Admittedly we react more deeply to beauty of mind and of expression, but when both beauty of mind and body are present we obtain complete satisfaction.

A work of art appeals to us in much the same way; we admire its shape, we are moved by its message. We are thrilled by a very stirring message even if it is presented in an ugly form. But what charms us most and leaves the deepest impression is a fine message enclosed in a beautiful form. All the great music of every period has these two essentials, in common with the great pictures, poems, buildings, and other works of art.

Form in music is more difficult for the ordinary person to appreciate than form in other arts. It cannot make its full impression unless the hearer has a certain amount of technical knowledge, a modicum of curiosity and interest, and a memory. But just as any one is to be pitied who experiences no delight from a fine specimen of humanity, a beautiful picture, poem, or building, so musicians feel sorry for people whose appreciation of music goes no further than its emotional message. To those who can conceive mentally the sound of a score of music, beautiful form brings a joy irrespective of actual sound. It is a thrill to look at it in cold print.

Let us now consider the form of a melody, for here we get the form of an extended movement in miniature. Melodies might be called the wild-flowers of music, for at any rate in the case of the oldest—folk-songs and ancient tunes—they originated from uncultivated soil. We are now going to examine some of these natural products in detail in order to perceive their beauties more fully.

The element which most readily appeals is the actual rise

29

and fall of the tune, its mountains and valleys, its climaxes and points of repose. The virtue of beautiful lines in a tune is obvious; for if it remained on one note throughout, or hung about one pitch, it would be monotonous, and if it dived up and down without rhyme or reason it would be incoherent and irritating. Naturally the position of the highest peak is also important, for unless it occurs in the middle or towards the end there will be a subsequent feeling of anticlimax.

The pleasantest and healthiest movement is in the form of waves; disagreeable shocks are then impossible. Moreover, curves are always the outcome of courage and enthusiasm. One cannot draw a curve timidly. The curve of a rallentando, an accelerando, a crescendo, or diminuendo, can only be perfectly reproduced by the expression of unselfconscious emotion. A row of artisans' dwellings, put up without thought of beauty, but only for material gain, is an exhibition of straight lines and angles; a great cathedral shows a vista of curve upon curve. There are numberless varieties of these curves both in music and other arts, some with gentle and unexciting rises and falls, others with a sudden rise or fall. But constant jumps in both directions are, as has been said, irritating. Here is the well-known 'Londonderry Air'. Most musicians agree that it is the finest folk-song in existence. For the moment consider merely its lovely curves, noting the position of its powerful climax, and the way this is gradually built up to by the two phrases that rise to E flat immediately before it.

40

Andante sostenuto

Many fine melodies rely entirely on their shape, the balance of their phrases and the position of their cadences; they have no other elements of form. Tunes had their origin in occupational cries, dances, and poetry. The primitive tunes which must gradually have taken the place of speech when the boatmen and sailors rowed or heaved up the anchor, or when the mother crooned her baby to sleep, were so short and involved so much repetition that they could not show much beauty of form. Much of the symmetry of the later tunes must have come from the dance and from poetry. They were made to fit either the steps of the dancers or the metre of the poems. A cadence ended the phrase of the tune where there was a break at the end of a figure of the dance or the end of a line of a poem. The arrangement of cadences has been the same for hundreds of years. The idea of first making a statement, then a slight excursion and a return to home, or somewhere near home, and then following this up with the most exciting section and finally returning home again, is found in thousands of tunes, just as it is found in thousands of stories. The commonest arrangement of cadences is: (1) Tonic (to fix the key definitely in our minds); (2) Dominant, or if the tune is in a minor mode or key, the relative major (an excursion to the nearest key); (3) Any other key—the free section (the most exciting part) and finally, (4) Tonic—home again. The order of (1) and (2) is often reversed. A few tunes are appended showing this order of cadences.[1]

41   English Folk Song 'High Germany'

[1] Folk-songs originally had no accompaniments and therefore no harmonized cadences: they came to rest on certain notes of the mode or scale at the end of the verbal phrases. But these notes very often followed the plan given above, as can be seen from the examples.

42   Manx Folk Song 'The Sheep under the Snow'

43 Melody of the second movement of Haydn's String quartet in D minor
Op.76, No.2.

Andante, più tosto Allegretto

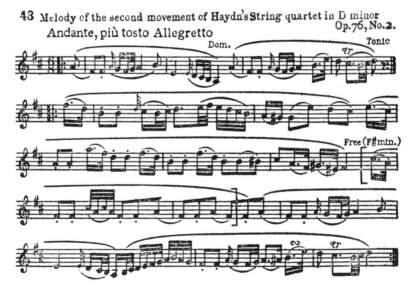

The two folk-songs are in the Aeolian mode, and must therefore be upwards of three hundred years old. 'The sheep under the snow' has the order of the two first cadences reversed (so has the Haydn tune). It has a closing group, or coda, of which more later on. The Haydn was written in the last quarter of the eighteenth century. It is much more of a cultivated garden flower—bigger, more ornate, and more cunningly

organized than the folk-tunes. But all three are founded on
the same idea, an establishment of the key, a short excursion,
another, more exciting, to some key further off, and a return
home. Later on it will be seen how this plan was followed in
more extended forms.

Works of art show characteristics which can be divided into
two groups: those imparting unity and those giving variety.
Widely speaking the unifying elements are common to all, like
the skeleton of the body, or the trunk and branches of a tree.
Some of them, like rhythmic patterns, have been common to
music of all time. They may have originated in the tunes made
from occupational cries. Others, like the progressions of
chords and the chords themselves, have periods or fashions
which change. Because they recur and are present in so much
music, people get accustomed to them and accept them as
constructive or fundamental elements. Each composer uses
what may be called the dry bones, and then clothes them with
his own imaginings, thus giving personality and variety to
his work.

Behind all music is a succession of pulses, beats, or throbs.
Without them music becomes vague and indefinite. Like day
and night, summer and winter, and like poetry, these pulsa-
tions alternate between heavy and light, between work and
rest. Sometimes there is one light beat between each heavy
beat, sometimes there are two. In making a tune there are
three options a composer can take: he can make his notes the
exact length of one beat, or he can write a sound exactly
covering two or more beats, or he can write notes of less than
a beat in length. The subdivisions are very numerous. If
notes no quicker than a quarter of a beat are used, the beat
can be split up in ten different ways.

44

If the syncopation obtained by tying a note of one beat on
to a note of the next, or if the subdivisions of the triplet are
included, the number is increased enormously. It is impos-

C

sible to calculate the permutations and combinations of all the rhythmic patterns and figures thus effected. One can find good tunes that have stood the test of time which have all three options separately or in combination. There are not many consisting entirely of notes exactly one beat in length, and most of these are hymn tunes. In Victorian times some of them had their original and varied rhythm ironed out, and were made very much duller and boring in the process. The Old Hundredth is a typical example; in Victorian times it was sung in minims:

45

etc.

Now it has recovered its ancient and far more interesting varied rhythm:

45(a)

etc.

Music being entirely dependent upon contrast, composers often affect monotony for a while in order that the delicious relief when it ends may be fully enjoyed. The germ of this effect, like so many other seeds which were to bear fruit later on, can be found in a melody. This folk-song, 'A farmer's son so sweet', has three monotonous crotchet phrases. They are quite worth while because of the charming contrast of the last one.

46

A tune consisting entirely of notes worth two beats or more would of course be too slow and monotonous. But there are

many which have no subdivisions of the beat. Here is one
that may be in this class if taken so slowly that there are un-
doubtedly three beats in a bar. The harmonization is by Bach.

47

Puer Natus   German 16th century tune

It may, however, be sung quickly, so that one of Bach's bars
becomes a beat, in which case every beat is subdivided into
notes which are alternately two-thirds and one-third of a beat:

48

If a clearly defined rhythmic pattern is largely used in a tune,
this will unify it and make it hang together intelligibly without
the inclusion of any other factor. A good example is the
principal subject of the slow movement of Beethoven's Fifth
Symphony.

But rhythmic figures are chiefly useful in another way, that
is, in repetitions. From time immemorial one of the chief
points of emotional interest in a tune, or in a more extended
piece, has been recapitulation—the return of a theme, or a

section of it, previously heard and liked. The same effect can be found in hundreds of tales—the return of the hero after every one has given him up for lost, as, for instance, in the story of the Prodigal Son. Our feelings are deliberately worked up by the author in order that the return may be doubly welcome. The same is true in music, which never gives people anything they intensely desire until their appetites have been sufficiently whetted. All this can be found in miniature in a melody, although it is too short to work up very much in the way of an exciting anticipation. (Cf. the section in square brackets in Ex. 43.) Any pleasure to be derived from a reprise depends upon the musical memory of the hearer; for if the likeness of the heio has been forgotten his return will not be recognized.

Rhythm makes a deeper impression on the memory than any other element in music. Tunes with incisive, arresting figures can be recognized from the rhythm alone. Test this by tapping out the rhythm of some well-known tune with a distinctive rhythm and observe how easily it is named.

It is for these reasons that we find so many tunes whose unity depends on repetition of some sort. Repetitions are used in two different ways; in some tunes whole phrases, and in others short figures or patterns are repeated.

The commonest of all musical forms is that expressed by A B A, where A is the first and principal section, and B is a contrasted section in another key. This form has been used for thousands of arias in opera, oratorio, and cantata, and for as many instrumental pieces. Most likely this form sprang from melody. In many cases such arias and pieces are simply two melodies lengthened out. Here is a German tune which dates back to the sixteenth century, if not earlier, according to Riemann, the German authority on ancient tunes. It is interesting because of its irregular bars, some of three beats, some of four; and its irregular phrase lengths consisting of five, three, two, and five bars. It has no climax, for it returns to D four times. It goes home to G too soon. But it is successful by reason of its rhythmic variety and because the recapitulation of the first phrase is varied. It is always more interesting if these repetitions are varied, provided the variation is more attractive than the original statement. Here it contains longer notes to bring the tune to a close.

49

The Secret Flower

Very often the first phrase of a melody is repeated, as in the old English tune, 'Drink to me only with thine eyes', or the folk-song, 'Green Bushes', where all three repetitions are varied, the second having a cadence on the fifth note of the mode.

50 Green Bushes

All these three concepts, the repeat at the start of the principal phrase, its final recapitulation, and its variation, found their way into sonata form and other forms, as will be seen further on. Cf. Ex. 1 (recapitulation) and Exs. 40 (all three), 41 (recapitulation), 43 (all three).

Various other forms of repetition of phrases can be found in melodies, some of which also have their prototypes in more extended pieces. A few examples are given below.

A B A C. English folk-song, 'Bruton Town', and the second subject of the last movement of Mozart's Piano Sonata in F (K332). The first two bars are given for reference.

51

Bruton Town

52

A B B C. Irish folk-song, 'The dear Irish Girl'.

53

A B B. English folk-song, 'Bushes and Briars'.

54

The use of the other type of repetition—the recurrence of a rhythmic pattern—leads to more variety than the repetition of whole phrases, for, as has been shown, there are endless possibilities in the invention of such figures, and many different ways of repeating them. They may repeat at the same pitch:

55

Slavonic Dance. Dvořàk

Or the repetition may be at a different pitch, as in the first
subject of the Adagio of Beethoven's Piano Sonata in C, op. 2,
no. 3. Again the repetition may be only of the rhythmic figure
and not of the intervals, as in Ex. 43. All three types may of
course occur in the same tune.

Another means of unification and cohesion is to repeat
some fairly large and distinctive interval in a melody, such as
a sixth, seventh, or octave. The five falling sixths and the single
fall of a seventh in the melody of Schubert's song, 'An die
Musik', and the dropping sixths and sevenths in the second
subject of the first movement of his Piano Trio in B flat,
op. 99, which begins like this:

56

are examples. The upward leap of a seventh or octave was
almost a mannerism with Elgar. The Committal theme from
The Dream of Gerontius, beginning thus:

57

Andantino

is a typical case. A similar result is obtained if a short succession of intervals is repeated. The C, B flat, and G which recur
six times, and the F, E flat, and C, forming the same intervals at

a different pitch, which recur three times in the Londonderry Air, Ex. 40, are a good example. The effect of unification is not lost even though the succession of notes occurs at different points in the phrases. Of course the originators of folk-songs were unaware of all this; in fact, the use of the pentatonic scale of five notes (F G A C D) or the hexatonic scale of six notes may have accounted for the repetitions. The Londonderry Air would be in a scale of six notes were it not for the single A flat in the seventh bar. But unity is achieved whether this is the case or not.

Play over the beautiful West Country folk-song, 'Matthew, Mark, Luke, and John', given below; and observe how unity is imparted to it by the recurrence of the succession of notes marked by slurs. Variety is obtained by avoiding the use of this succession in the same position in the phrase, except when the last phrase is repeated.

58

All these various devices to be found in ancient tunes were destined to reappear as means of development in more extended music hundreds of years later.

It has been said that the form of a melody is closely linked with the metre of poetry. This, together with nature's law that work and repose must alternate, is the reason why the phrase-lengths of music are so often of two, four, or eight bars. This can easily lead to monotony and four-squareness, especially when the rhythmic divisions and the shape are not very interesting. Melodies are relieved of this stiffness by devices that came originally from speech. Just as we dwell on important syllables in speaking poetry even when we interrupt the flow of the metre by doing so, composers lengthen out important notes such as climaxes, even when this means an extra beat in a bar, or an extra bar in a phrase. Ex. 53, for instance, has five bars instead of four in the last phrase. Another example will be found in the first subject of Brahms's Fourth Symphony (Ex. 68). In speaking a poem we should not wait at the end of a line for the exact time to elapse to make one line the same length as the others. So in music many phrases which finish on the first beat of four in a bar are followed immediately by the next phrase, without waiting for two beats to elapse. This happens in Bach's version of 'Puer natus', Ex. 47, but here the time is 3/4. Compare the seventh bar of Ex. 47 with the second bar of Ex. 48. In 'The Bold Fisherman', an English folk-song, given below, the fourth bar should have had five beats if the phrases were to be both the same length.

59

In instrumental tunes these helps to variety also occur, and there is one other—the repeat of a figure to emphasize it, even when this makes an extra bar. This happens in the fourth phrase of the Haydn tune (Ex. 43), in fact almost every point referred to is to be found in this little tune, which sounds so naïve but is so wonderfully moulded. This device must have come from speech in which repetition is a common form of emphasis. Nature never makes an absolutely straight line, a perfect circle, sphere, or square. These tunes with irregular bars and phrase-lengths—ungeometrical tunes, so to speak—have a natural charm all their own.

In conclusion let us make up a tune for ourselves. It shall have words, for these will give us ideas of rhythm and shape, and fix the number of phrases and their length. Let us make a tune to 'Mary had a little lamb'. It shall be as simple as the poem. The important points are, first that the lamb was white, and second, that it never failed to accompany Mary.

Version one grasps these ideas, but has a very dull rhythm and too much repetition without variation:

60

Ma-ry had a   lit-tle lamb, Its fleece was white as snow; And

ev - ry-where where Ma-ry went, The lamb was sure to   go.

Let us give it the appropriate pastoral lilt by changing it to 6/8 time:

60 (a)

Now it has a rhythmic pattern of a very common order. But it is still monotonous. Let us try the effect of a couple of passing notes to relieve the sameness, and lengthen out the notes on the important syllables:

60 (b)

Finally let us relieve the tune of any monotony that still remains by changing a note in the second bar, which only duplicates the first, and by making two of the four falling fourths into fifths:

60 (c)

It is to be hoped that in the light of what has been explained readers will now amuse themselves by writing melodies. It is of greater import, however, that all should appreciate how much music owes to folk-tunes and ancient melodies of all sorts.

III

LET us now trace the development of instrumental forms during the seventeenth and the first half of the eighteenth centuries. From this it will be seen how sonata form—the greatest of all—had its origin, and why certain forms are dead and forgotten while others have lived.

First let us endeavour to put ourselves in the shoes of the composers who flourished between 1550 and 1600. Up till then the Church had complete control of all serious music. At a time when few could read or write, still fewer could read or write music, and these were all priests or church musicians. The folk-singers and primitive instrumentalists who played for the dancing, sang and played by the light of nature. After the Renaissance it gradually became fashionable to practise domestic music. First the lute and viol and then keyed instruments such as the clavichord, virginals, spinet, and harpsichord became popular, and music was demanded and written for them.[1] Contemporary composers were fascinated by the ease with which a good player could run up and down a well-made keyed instrument, and when the violin gradually supplanted the older viol as the seventeenth century advanced, they were charmed with the new technique of this wonderful instrument, and with the way it could draw the heart out of a melody.

Then came the revival of opera, due to the spread of education and the study of the classical authors. It was found that the Greeks had music for their plays, and in 1602 the first Italian opera was written by Peri and Caccini. The delicate tones of the clavichord, spinet, and virginals by themselves were of little use as an accompaniment to opera. Thus the orchestra came into being.

Now the situation can be understood—better instruments, opera, and a demand for chamber or domestic music: composers delighted with the facility with which the new instruments could be played, but with no experience of how to write for them: men who could turn out a glorious mass, motet, or

---

[1] The clavichord was in existence in 1400. Records and pictures of the other three are found early in the sixteenth century.

madrigal, but who might quite logically have regarded the popular dance tunes as something rather beneath them. What they wrote in the way of instrumental music was pretty much what one would expect. They knew that their vocal music was a finished, cultured, and satisfying art-form. And therefore, just as the first fashioners of railway carriages and motor-cars took the best horse-drawn vehicles as their models, late sixteenth- and early seventeenth-century composers used the form of the motet and madrigal in writing instrumental pieces. Some of these were labelled 'apt for voices or viols'; others had embellishments which were impossible to sing, but otherwise were written in the same form as the vocal music. But that form had been determined by the words. A theme was written for each sentence and this was treated contrapuntally. Each voice entered successively with the theme, and it was thrown about from one voice to another until its resources were worked out. Then followed the next sentence in the text and it was given the same treatment. Occasionally a phrase was harmonized in block chords as a contrast to the woven strands of counterpoint. But as each section had a different theme, there was nothing to unify these fantasias, or 'fancies' as they were called; they rambled on and never seemed to get anywhere, although the individual sections were often very beautiful. It was the words that had previously made the music coherent; without them it fell into isolated divisions.

It was not the counterpoint that was to blame. In later times it was discovered that two or three themes used *throughout* a piece were much more likely to hold attention and stimulate emotion, for they could be presented in different lights with a gradual accumulation of interest and excitement. Thus the fugue was gradually developed. It was over a hundred years before it reached its zenith in the time of Bach.

Meanwhile, composers had other forms to experiment with, namely, those which exploited the newly acquired facility in playing rapid passages, and those which were concerned with expanding and elaborating the secular folk and dance tunes. The first type—the toccatas[1] and preludes of the period— sound very empty and meaningless to our ears. But that also was to be expected. A new invention has at first an interest and charm in itself and by itself, apart from its ultimate

[1] Latin, *toccare*, to touch.

usefulness. (Many can remember when the wireless was so much of a wonder that to listen to sounds coming apparently from nowhere was quite enough to thrill the listener irrespective of what was actually being broadcast.) This accounts for the number of pieces written at the beginning of the seventeenth century which consisted entirely of *bravura*, or, as a rather illiterate pupil used to call them, 'bravado' passages. Unfortunately the worship of technical acrobatics still persists. Audiences are still fascinated with them, and some composers are still guilty of writing music which, if stripped of this glittering robe, has little else to recommend it. A short prelude by Byrd (d. 1623) illustrates this point perfectly.[1] Although these early attempts have little interest for us, yet they were useful, for they taught musicians how to write decorative passages which were to be of importance in building up extended movements in later days.

The folk-song and the dance, rather crudely set out to begin with, were to have a far greater influence on form. As the differently coloured chords of harmony began to have an emotional effect, since the major and minor keys had superseded the modes, what could be more natural than to harmonize a tune in different ways? Then says the composer to himself, 'I like all these different harmonizations. Why not combine them all in one work, obtaining contrast by varying the amount of movement in each, as well as by varying the harmony and the melody?' Singers of Folk-songs have always shown a delight in embellishing tunes with fanciful turns and grace notes. Perhaps it was this habit that led to the decoration of the theme itself Even in the earliest variations all three methods are present: varied harmony, melody, and movement. It was a long time before anything further was attempted, but in the end the art was carried so far that in some modern variations it is impossible to detect the tune, which is only the constructional element, like the steel girders in a modern building.

Two courses are now open to us: either we can examine the first attempts and leave modern developments until later, or we can follow the progress of each form through the centuries and compare the music. The latter plan seems far more useful and interesting. We will therefore compare three sets of varia-

---

[1] Refer to the list of music for the illustrations.

tions: Byrd's on 'The Carman's Whistle', Mozart's on *Unser dummer Pöbel meint*, and Brahms's on a theme by Handel.

Variations on 'The Carman's Whistle', by Byrd. Before the theme Byrd writes four bars, consisting of the first two bars of the theme, as a solo imitated in the next two a fifth lower. This was prophetic, and must have been one of the earliest examples of what in later years grew to much greater proportions—the introduction, the call to attention. The theme is very simple, and consists of two two-bar melodic figures, the first twice repeated, and the second four times with different endings. In the first variation the theme is decorated, the second half quite cunningly, for the decoration begins on the last crotchet of the previous bar, thus making the phrase iambic instead of trochaic like the others. The harmony is different from that of the theme, but quite as simple. The second variation has two little countersubjects, one at bar 5 and the other (at bar 9) in close imitation between the lower parts. The cross-rhythm in the first four bars is not a novelty, for such devices were used by Byrd and his contemporaries in their vocal music. The next three variations are on the same plan; countersubjects are written against the theme. The fourth and fifth have more movement, and in the fifth the decorated version of the theme itself is used as a countersubject. In the sixth there is less movement by way of contrast, and a new feature appears in a sequential series of suspensions. The seventh has a quicker movement than any, and a running bass which contains the idea of a rhythmic figure used as an accompaniment. This was to be widely used in later days, as for, instance, in the songs of Schubert. The Finale is most interesting. The theme is first in an inner part, then disappears, a point of imitation taking its place over the same harmony as that of the theme. Many hundreds of variations have since been written on this plan, that is, discarding the melody of the theme but retaining its harmonic structure. At the ninth bar a startling diversion is caused by a sudden change to the key of D minor. The actual theme would not fit with this, for it ends on C natural. This modulation is repeated in the next bar, but in a different way.

This set of variations is therefore remarkable: (1) for the introduction, (2) for the way the theme is decorated, (3) for the use of countersubjects, (4) for the early appreciation of rhythmic contrast, and (5) for the finale which anticipates the modern free variation.

Variations on ' Unser dummer Pöbel meint', by Mozart. These date from 1784, and have therefore a much richer harmonic scheme, far more rhythmic variety, and more individual character. But still, after upwards of a hundred and fifty years, the three methods of variation used by Byrd are found. In the third bar of the first variation a departure is made from the theme, but the basic harmony is retained. The first two variations both contain examples of reiterated rhythmic figures. The third transforms the naïve and heavy tune into a delicate, girlish movement. The fourth begins with the theme in octaves in the bass, the right hand coming down with a crash on a chord which harmonizes the last note. This chord varies with each repetition, becoming more unexpected every time. It is followed by a hearty ripple of laughter! In the fifth and sixth the first phrase of the theme, instead of repeating the notes of the descending scale, goes down in chromatic semitones. This leads to chromatic harmony. Mozart always knew when and how to use this. Notice that in number five the middle section of the theme is omitted, and four bars are inserted developing the countersubject. The seventh goes back to the diatonic version of the theme but retains the chromatic harmony. The eighth divides the theme between the lowest and the uppermost part, two notes at a time, and passes without break into a cadenza calculated to make us feel that something important is coming and that its entry must therefore be delayed until our appetites are whetted. The ninth variation does not disappoint us. It is an adagio, but even so the theme is spread over twice as many bars as at its first appearance. This makes the variation about four times as long as its predecessors. The spaces thus created are filled with decorations of the most graceful character, replete with rhythmic variety. The Finale, beginning with an allegro variation in triple time leading into another cadenza and then into a long coda founded on the theme, offers exactly the right contrast to the Adagio and brings the work to a most satisfying conclusion. There is so much individual character in each of these variations that one could almost imagine that Mozart was giving us a musical portrayal of the personality of his friends, as Elgar did in his 'Enigma' Variations.

Variations on a Theme by Handel, by Brahms, op. 24. Here is the skeleton of the theme, stripped of its few ornaments:

61

Prospective composers of variations will do well to observe its extreme simplicity. An ornate theme is not the best type for variations, for it is itself a variation. It is in two-part form, the first part coming to rest on the dominant chord and the second starting from that point and coming back to the tonic. This skeleton was behind the composer's mind constantly, for there are but few references to the passing notes at the third crotchets of the first three bars of each phrase,[1] and still fewer to the flourishes which conclude each half.[2] The basic harmony is scarcely altered in eight variations[3] and many of the others start with it, but have charming diversions to other keys as they proceed. It is only necessary to glance at each variation to know the secret of success of this work—it is crammed full of rhythmic invention. Sometimes the same idea is used for consecutive variations,[4] but even then the treatment is so different that a complete contrast is achieved. The recipe is as follows: Take the basic harmony and the general shape of the melody stripped of its ornaments, and invent rhythmic figures which can be made to follow the course of either or both. They must be attractive and fully alive, and be arranged in a sequence that will give plenty of contrast, and yet accumulate interest to the end. Variations 9, 17, and 18 should be

[1] Variations 6, 7, 14, 15, 16, 22, and the fugue.
[2] Variations 1, 10, 13, and 25.
[3] Variations 1, 5, 10, 12, 14, 22, 24, and 25.
[4] Variations 5 and 6; 7 and 8; 14, 15, and 16; 23 and 24.

D

examined carefully. In No. 9 Brahms takes the skeleton of the first phrase of the theme, using the chromatic instead of the diatonic scale for the second half of it, and then builds up the whole of the variation on this idea alone; the rest of the theme does not appear, but a kinship with it is maintained by retaining the two-part form. Even this is freshly treated, for although the first half ends on the dominant with a repeat, the repetition of the second is varied, for it is carried into a new and unexpected key from which it returns in a masterly way at the last two bars. Nos. 17 and 18 are constructed in much the same way. Here only the first four notes of the theme are used. They are given to the tenor part, whilst the right hand has a charming staccato figure as a counter-attraction. In No. 18 this counter-theme becomes a rippling arpeggio figure, and instead of being confined to the top part is thrown about between left and right hands. The final fugue is unconventional and contains more thematic development than counterpoint. It makes a wonderful conclusion to the work.

Variation form came into being in the very early days of instrumental music; it still holds its own. The reason is not far to seek, for this form allows great freedom for the play of the composer's imagination and powers of development. Stanford, perhaps our greatest teacher of composition, made his students practise it assiduously.

Another form that had its origin in the early days of the seventeenth century and is still in use is the suite, a series of dances arranged in a certain order. The two which first made their appearance were the Pavan and the Galliard, the most popular of the period. The only attempt at order was to follow the stately Pavan with the merry Galliard. Thus it was soon perceived that human nature demands the serious before the gay. Gradually the number of dances increased. Almans, Almaines, or Allemandes (of German origin, as the title implies) were written in the first quarter of the century, and others soon followed. These dances always had a two-part or binary form. The earlier ones only differ in form from some of the melodies given in the last chapter in that each half is repeated. At first each half had a cadence on the tonic, but the convention of making the first half finish on the dominant was soon established. To begin with, composers had not learned how to develop a tune; their only means of extension was by repetition. The earliest settings of dances were written just at the time when the old ecclesiastical modes were being superseded by the modern major and minor scales. Gradually it began to dawn on composers that a refreshing contrast could be obtained by change of key. Instead of making the sections end with cadences on various notes of the mode, the music was placed in a key at a different pitch altogether and allowed to remain there for an appreciable time. In the earlier dances the second half had nothing to do with the first. Later on it was found that far more unity could be obtained if the theme of the first part was retained in the second with a change of key. When the binary form became crystallized it was the custom to begin the second part with a restatement of the theme in the dominant key, or the relative major if the original key was minor. One more interesting and prophetic development gradually appeared. It was discovered that if the cadence, more or less elaborated, at the end of part one was repeated at the end of part two, another point of unity was secured. Eventually this idea was extended until it became the closing group or codetta of sonata form.

The following selection of dances shows how they grew from simple tunes at the beginning of the seventeenth century to satisfying art-forms in the time of Bach.

Pavan, '*The Earl of Salisbury*', *Byrd*. The composer cannot refrain from putting in some scholarly, church-like imitation and cross-rhythm. The same arrangement of cadences will be noticed as was so often found in the melodies in the previous chapter—tonic, dominant, some new key, and back to the tonic. There is no development—just the plain tune, and no referring back or repetition except the repeat of each half.

Almaine, *Gibbons* (1583–1625). Each half finishes in the same key; the short excursion to the dominant occurs in the middle of part one. But a real change of key is made in part two. The final bars of both parts have just enough resemblance to give a tiny bit of unity to the piece.

Almand in C, *Purcell* (1656–95). By the time this was written things had moved along considerably. Both parts are much longer, especially the second. There is a closing group of four bars to round off each part. The second part begins with the same rhythmic figure as the first. The syncopated figure which forms the closing group is developed for a few bars in the second part. The music, instead of having cadences on certain notes, definitely modulates to the dominant at the close of the first part, and to A minor and F in the second.

Courante in G from the Fifth French Suite, Bach. This dance shows the progress made in the art of development. The first five bars contain all the thematic material. The form is the usual ancient binary in its crystallized form, with a closing group of four bars constructed from bars 2 and 3 (R.H.) and a re-statement of the theme in the dominant to begin the second part.

The arrangements of these dance movements in the suite foreshadowed the sequence of movements in the sonatas and symphonies of later times. The more intellectual, of fairly quick pace, came first, such as the allemande and courante. Sometimes the suite began with a long prelude. Then followed the slow and often deeply moving sarabande. Next in order were the attractive and stimulating gavottes and minuets. The jolly, carefree gigue nearly always ended the suite. The opening dances corresponded in sentiment and place to the allegro of the sonata, the sarabande to the slow movement. The idea of using a couple of short dances like the minuet for the third section was continued right up to the time of Beethoven. The final rondo of the sonata was often in the same jolly mood as the gigue.

It was natural that the seventeenth-century musicians should prefer to have some fixed basis or form upon which to found their work. The art was young, and they needed a convenient framework to guide them even more than we do. Such a framework was the 'ground-bass'. This was a short figure repeated continuously as a bass. Above it the composer showed his harmonic and contrapuntal skill by inventing all manner of variations. The two movements (originally dances) known as the 'chaconne' and the 'passacaglia', were written in this way. The form needs no explanation. Originally the theme was confined to the bass, but later on, as in the two movements just-referred to, monotony was avoided by transferring it to other parts and sometimes to other keys. A few classical examples are given below.

Dido's Lament from the Opera 'Dido and Aeneas', by Purcell. Purcell was a master of this form. He wrote many fine examples of which this is the best known. The accompaniment was written by Purcell himself, not as a figured bass, but for the strings of the orchestra. The rich, expressive, varied harmony and the dramatic part for the voice are the most noteworthy features. The ground-bass is formed, like that of several other celebrated examples, from the descending notes of the chromatic scale.

Ciaccona for violin and figured bass by Tommaso Vitali (end of the seventeenth century). The accompaniment has been added by a modern editor. The ground-bass (the first four notes of the descending scale of G minor) repeats no less than forty-eight times, but the many different figures given to the violin, and also the way the bass itself is split up into various figures, prevent any sense of monotony. Some of the variations are in quite remote keys reached by quick and clever modulations. The piece has a fine general architectural scheme, with the big towers in just the right places, the grandest being reserved for the end.

Passacaglia in C minor for organ, by Bach (1685–1750). Here, as in Vitali's work, the bass is sometimes split up into figures and sometimes transferred to other parts than the bass. The form, which is normal, is not so much importance as the colossal grandeur of the music.

Chaconne for Violin alone, by Bach. This forms the finale of the Second Partita for violin solo. It has even more depth and power than the organ work. A single violin seems incapable of drawing forth all the great message of the music, despite Bach's genius in arranging it for that instrument. There are sixty-four variations with either a definite perfect cadence or cadential harmony at the end of each one. The miracle is that the music always carries us along despite the full stops. Here also the bass is often split up, modified, or merely implied.

Crucifixus, from the Mass in B minor, Bach. The ground-bass consists of the first six notes of the descending chromatic scale of E minor. It is repeated without alteration throughout, with imitative parts for the chorus above it accompanied by a figure for flutes very suggestive of weeping. The effect of the close, where the key is changed to G, the orchestra ceases except for the basses, and the chorus sinks into a tense pianissimo, is amongst the most poignant moments in all music.

Bach thus chose the ground-bass as a means to convey three of the most remarkable manifestations of his genius.

Allegro energico e passionato, from the Fourth Symphony in

E minor, op. 98, *by Brahms.* Brahms sums up in this movement all previous ground-basses, chaconnes, and passacaglias. He is not trammelled by convention—he even alters the length of the theme in some cases. He uses his outstanding gift of writing variations in decorating the theme and inventing counter-themes. He never allows the movement to flag or falter by avoiding actual cadences, although the last two notes of the theme form the bass of the perfect cadence. By altering the tempo and changing the mood from Variation 12 to Variation 15, and leaving the key of E minor for that of E major, he forms a distinct and separate middle section and creates the feeling of recapitulation when the theme returns in its original form and key at Variation 16. In addition to the sense of unity generated by the repetitions of the theme in various forms, still more homogeneity is imparted by the re-introduction in the final section of counter-themes originally heard in the first. Compare Variations 25 and 26 with Variation 3. After thirty variations the movement is brought to a most exciting close by a coda chiefly constructed from the diminution[1] of the theme. Having so carefully avoided the perfect cadence up to this point, there is little wonder that the composer should hammer down the key of E minor with no less than six perfect cadences as a conclusion.

There are two ways in which opera contributed to musical form, for it was through opera that the overture and the aria came into being.

Aria form was the first example of three-part, or ternary form. It is still the commonest of all, for literally thousands of short instrumental pieces have been written in it. It consists of a first section coming to a conclusion in the key from which it started, and complete in itself, a middle part in a contrasted key and a different mood, then a da capo of the first part. This note-for-note repetition seems rather trying to modern ears; a throw back, so that the listener is no further on emotionally at the end of the piece than he was at the end of part one. This weakness has been overcome in the more modern use of the form by making the repeat more interesting in some way, so as to throw a new light on the theme, or by shortening it, and by adding a coda.[2]

[1] See p. 60.
[2] Aria form has already been seen in embryo in Examples 1, 40 and 43, and in the theme of Mozart's Variations.

The overture began in a small way as a short prelude. If it was of any length it was fugal, for it was not until the century was well advanced that a long movement was evolved not entirely dependent upon counterpoint. The order of the movements varied in the French and Italian overtures. The French began with a slow and solemn introduction, whilst the Italians commenced with an allegro. The principal movement, when it was not fugal, had much the same form as the longer movements of the concertos of the period. The concerto, however, presented one important difference, namely the statement of the theme by the full orchestra followed by its repetition by the solo instrument, or by a group of solo instruments. The late Sir Donald Tovey said the idea was taken from the vocal aria. This is probably true. The aria of opera and oratorio begins with a loud statement of the theme by the orchestra. The soloist then repeats it accompanied by the harpsichord and an obbligato instrument, or by a reduced orchestra. A very effective means of contrast is thus obtained.

It is obvious that the longer the movement the more necessity there is for contrast. Music abounds in contrasts—high and low, loud and soft, quick and slow, discord and concord. But the most effective if rightly used is the contrast of one rhythmic figure, or one complete theme, with another. Two colours may be so much alike that if placed in proximity they both lose their effect. Two contrasting colours may act as a foil to each other, or they may clash horribly. It is the same with themes in music; they may be too similar to have any effect, they may set each other off, or they may not suit one another in the least. In the period we are considering, the end of the seventeenth and the beginning of the eighteenth centuries, very little of this was known. Contrasts of vocal and instrumental parts in counterpoint, of concord and discord, of a small body of instruments with the full orchestra, of high and low, of loud and soft, of one whole movement with another, are to be found, but not of themes and rhythms in the same movement.

The general plan of these longer movements is as follows: the themes are more of the contrapuntal than the harmonic type, that is, short, easily remembered rhythmic groups suitable for appearance in any part including the bass. The later composers, Corelli (1653–1713), Vivaldi (d. 1743), Purcell, Handel (1685–1751), and Bach, developed these themes and their component rhythms at some length. Speaking broadly the texture is contrapuntal; each voice has an important part to play and does not merely fill up the harmony. The form is an extension of the binary form already described. This has one main division, but the longer movements have more. The first ends, as in binary, on the dominant or relative major, and sometimes in the original key. The following divisions end with cadences in other related keys such as the relative minor and subdominant. Often the closing phrase is the same at the end of each section, as in binary form. Sections are often constructed from secondary themes, but these move at much the same pace as the principal theme. It should be noted that there are two methods by which the pace of music may be varied. Rallentandos and accelerandos may be used to slow up or quicken the beat or pulse, or the length of the notes themselves may be altered; for instance, minims may take the place of quavers, but the pace of the beat is in these cases unaltered. In the music of this period there is very little change of note-pace; the music moves at the same stride throughout. Frequently there is a repetition of the principal subject at the end, but not of any secondary theme.

There are many examples of such movements as these which are well known to all. Pianists will find them in Bach's Italian Concerto, or in the preludes to the English Suites, violinists in the longer movements of Corelli's and Vivaldi's concertos and in the sonatas of Handel, and organists in the preludes to Bach's organ fugues and in Handel's concertos.

To sum up: the seventeenth century saw the birth of instrumental form. The two-part form in which the earlier dance tunes were written began as a melody with each of its halves repeated. This form gradually expanded until it was crystallized in the ancient binary form. This in its turn was extended into the longer movements written at the end of the seventeenth and the beginning of the eighteenth centuries, when the art of development and the employment of secondary themes, or episodes, became known. Thus melody was the mother of them all.

IV

THE FUGUE AND THE CHORAL PRELUDE

WE now come to the consideration of counterpoint. Perhaps the best way of realizing the essential difference between contrapuntal music and the music which sprang from the dance and from song is through Dr. Colles's comparison of the former with a sermon and the latter with a story. There are many people who are shy about counterpoint and have a deep-seated objection to what they consider its dullness; they have not perceived that an able preacher can move his hearers quite as deeply as a fine story-teller. Dr. Colles's comparison was made because a contrapuntal piece has only one or two short themes, or subjects, like the text of a sermon, and because the success of both sermon and contrapuntal music depends upon the way the themes are treated and combined with other subsidiary ideas, the way in which they return after episodes during which, perhaps, a section of them is discussed or developed, and the skill which is employed to make the interest cumulative right up to the final peroration. The sonata-movement, or story, has more themes, usually of greater length and of very varied feeling and rhythm. These, like the characters and scenes in a story, are first announced in the exposition and then made to pass through more or less exciting adventures in the development, and finally appear at the end in the principal key or tonic, like the return of the hero in the story. Themes in this type of music are often in the upper part, the lower parts being mainly occupied in providing the harmonies. Thus is it that sonatas and the like are often spoken of as exhibiting the vertical aspect of music whilst counterpoint is certainly the horizontal one. This is not universally true of sonata movements, for they often have a horizontal interest, that is, the rhythmic life and continuity carry one forward, and hold the attention. In contrapuntal pieces, however, if each voice, instrument, or part is examined, it will be found to be as important and as interesting as any of the others. This is by no means so in the sonata movement, where some of the parts are often concerned with nothing more important than supplying the harmony and keeping the piece on the move by means of some rhythmic figure.

Imitation is the technical term used when two or more voices sing the same tune, but not at the same time. Even at the dawn of concerted vocal music it seems to have attracted the composer. Perhaps this contrapuntal device has more charm for the composer and the performer than for the listener. No doubt there is a thrill for a singer or instrumentalist in biding his time, listening to others giving out the theme, and finally, at the appropriate moment, getting his chance to interweave his thread in the texture. It is always an exciting moment to the solo performer when the theme enters, but when it thunders out at the peroration on the pedal reeds of an organ, or in octaves on the resonant bass of a grand piano, that is the biggest thrill of all. For the listener there are disturbing factors. In vocal music imitation means that all parts are often singing different words simultaneously, and it takes a very wide-awake ear to follow closely all the lines of the counterpoint. Despite these natural drawbacks, counterpoint and imitation found their way into Church music as early as the first quarter of the twelfth century.

It took many years for composers and theorists to discover what sounded convincing and sane in counterpoint, and what sounded ill-fitting and clumsy. It was a slow and gradual process. But the magnetic attraction of imitation was always powerful. In fact Church music at times became so involved that the authorities objected on the ground that the words of the mass and the motet were obscured by the complicated counterpoint.

One of the devices practised by composers even as early as the first half of the thirteenth century was 'canon',[1] a piece in which every part sings the same music commencing one after the other. This was originally called 'fugue',[2] because each voice flew or retreated before the ensuing voice which never caught it. The word 'canon' referred to the rules or laws which governed the composition. At first these terms, fugue and canon, were applied indiscriminately to what we should call a canon. Later on the word canon was reserved for the type of piece I have described, and the title of fugue was given to more extended movements the form of which we shall discuss presently.

In Chapter III attention was drawn to the seventeenth-cen-

[1] From Greek *Kanon*, a rule.   [2] From Latin *fuga*, a flight.

tury fantasy, a form successful as a motet, because the words gave it continuity and unity, but unsuccessful as an instrumental fantasy because each section sounded like a separate piece. Now every fugue begins with what is called an exposition. In this exposition exactly the same thing takes place as in the motet and the fantasy, that is, each part makes its entry with the subject. Here is the commencement of a motet written in the first quarter of the sixteenth century by J. Mouton of the Netherlands School.

62

Many people would call this a fugue. The reason it is not is that, after the excerpt quoted, the subject is not heard again. This section is merely a *point* or *punctus*, of which more anon.

Another good example is the beginning of a Fantasia or Fancy by Byrd. His *point* is considerably longer, and he introduces strettos, where one part enters with the subject before the previous entry is completed. But when his *point* is finished he never refers to his subject again.

Thus the motet and the fancy gave to the fugue its commencement, or exposition. As the fancies became less 'apt for voices or viols', and more instrumental in texture, so did the fugue subjects; although the suitability of this form for the solemn organ had a restraining influence, and the vocal type of subject persisted alongside the more florid and quicker instrumental type right down to the days of J. S. Bach. But composers soon began to discover that even when a slow and solemn theme was adopted, quicker instrumental counter-subjects could be introduced, sometimes at the beginning, and sometimes during the course of the fugue, to give contrast or to quicken the interest and excitement as the fugue progressed.

Contrapuntal devices such as strettos, already referred to, inversions, where all the intervals in a tune are reversed or turned upside down, augmentations and diminutions, where the time-values of the notes in the theme are proportionately lengthened and shortened respectively, were all known and practised by composers of the early seventeenth century. But there is a long gap between a discovery and the complete comprehension of all the uses to which it may be put. Take the internal combustion-engine, for instance. Some of us remember its first noisy and uncertain splutterings. No one dreamed in those days that in fifty years it would be propelling aeroplanes at the rate of four hundred miles an hour. At first the new discovery is quite attractive enough in itself without a thought of its ultimate usefulness. To illustrate this point, two fugues by composers of the early seventeenth century will be compared with two of Bach's which employ the same general principles of construction. The latter show how Bach used contrapuntal devices with a clear understanding of the effect they would have on the composition as a whole, and of their emotional effect upon the listener; whilst the two composers of about one hundred years earlier were evidently quite satisfied with these devices for their own sakes.

The first fugue is by Sweelinck (1562–1621). He is generally accepted as the greatest of the Dutch musicians. He was an organist, and this fugue, written for that instrument, was probably the first fully developed and extended composition in that form. From an historical point of view it is remarkable; but as normal music it is not very satisfying to the listener. The reason for this is apparent. Music is first and last a transmutation of human feelings and emotions into the beautiful and mysterious medium of sound. Take away the human element, so that no adjectives such as joyous, sad, solemn, stark, calm, or agitated could be applied to it, and its appeal to you and me is nil. Very often the pioneers and experimentalists are so much absorbed in their own discoveries that they forget the effect these novelties make on the emotions of their audience, and are quite content to play with their new toy irrespective of it. Now you will agree that our feelings change gradually. Take an instance of this from a child, for he presents no complications. He tumbles down and cuts his knee. The shock, the pain, and the sight of blood frighten him, and he cries bitterly. His mother binds up his wounds, takes him on her lap, gives him a sweet or two and shows him a picture-book. The sobs do not stop abruptly: they subside gradually and are followed gradually by smiles of content. This is not an argument against sudden changes in music. There are many that give us pleasure and arouse excitement, just as there are in life. You would not object to the shock of having left to you a fortune of which you had no expectation, or a sudden relief from some impending tragedy, or the quick turn of the road revealing a glorious vista. What you dislike is to walk into a doorpost in the blackout, or to find yourself with a puncture on a dark wet night when you are in a hurry, or to hear that your friend is dangerously ill. To return to Sweelinck's fugue: he evidently had an intuition that if he introduced quicker passages as it progressed, they would tend to whip up the excitement. But he had not the foresight to do this gradually and progressively. He jerks us off our feet with a burst of semiquavers as early as the ninth bar, and introduces two more similar shocks in the course of his opening, which originally set out to be solemn and dignified. Presently there is a flourish of quicker notes still—demisemiquavers—presumably to call attention to a well-written stretto in which all four voices join. This might have succeeded if the flourish had preceded the stretto, but two parts have already made their entries before the flourish, which is consequently distracting. Moreover, the stretto itself is all in minims and slows up the movement instead of making it more exciting. The middle section introduces three new countersubjects, but each one is put in a water-tight compartment: it is heard a few times and then disappears for good. The last countersubject is combined with an augmentation of the theme. But the semibreves are so prolonged that it is difficult to recognize the original tune. The most exciting section follows with semiquavers accompanying the diminution of the subject, first in quadruplets, then in sextolets. But even here there is something wanting, for the rapid passages simply run wildly up and down without any definite pattern to give point to them and make a real countersubject. The coda, or conclusion, is quite effective with its stretto and its two extended cadences, one perfect and the other plagal.

The other early fugue, or string of fugues, is by the great Italian organist Frescobaldi, who flourished twenty years later than Sweelinck. He was organist of St. Peter's, Rome. This piece is another attempt to keep the interest alive by beginning simply, and gradually adding more and more complications. He starts with a plain, normal fugue in A minor without a countersubject. This finishes with a cadence on the dominant. It is followed by another short fugue on a new subject which, however, has no more movement in it than its predecessor. This comes to a conclusion in the key of C major. The third fugue has the subject of the first one with the subject of the second as countersubject. Still the amount of movement is the same. This concludes in the original key of A minor and is followed by a fourth fugue on the original subject but in twelve-eight time. There is a secondary theme partly in semiquavers, but it is never combined with the subject. It has a faint likeness to the countersubject in the last section of the St. Anne Fugue by Bach which we shall presently discuss. The weaknesses in Frescobaldi's suite of fugues are first that each of the four is a separate movement, so that the listener begins each one from zero as far as interest is concerned, and secondly that by the time the second fugue is completed the theme of the first one has been forgotten.

Let us compare these two somewhat primitive fugues with two fugues by Bach: first the F sharp minor from the second book of the Forty-eight Preludes and Fugues which he called the *Well-tempered Clavier*, henceforward to be referred to as the 'Forty-eight'; second the great St. Anne Fugue in E flat for the organ, so-called in England because the subject is the same as the first phrase of our hymn-tune, St. Anne.

Like Sweelinck's, the F sharp minor is a continuous fugue and, like his, has more than one countersubject—two in fact. Both these are given separate expositions before being combined with the subject, so that we shall become thoroughly acquainted with them, and thus get the benefit of the pleasurable surprise when they are combined. Bach's expositions on his countersubjects are just the right length, not so long that we forget the original subject as in Frescobaldi's work, nor so short that we have no time to absorb the new tune. The second countersubject has more movement than the first, and this movement never flags or disappoints us by pulling us up short. It is not till quite near the end that Bach gives us subject and both countersubjects combined. Notice how closely he sticks to his texts. Even the voices not concerned in subject or countersubject are constructed from them. Even the drop of a fifth in the second bar of the subject is used for this purpose. The reiterated figure of three quavers is the inversion of the first three notes of the subject. The St. Anne Fugue, like Frescobaldi's, is a fugue in separate sections, but, unlike his, though each section finishes with a well-defined cadence, the succeeding one begins at once without pause or break. Again, as in the F sharp minor Fugue, he gives us an exposition on the new countersubject before combining it with the original subject. Like Sweelinck's and the F sharp minor there is more movement in each successive section. Here again Bach never lets it flag as Sweelinck does. His last countersubject does not run in notes of equal length, but has an attractive and easily recognized rhythmic figure. Notice how the episodes lead up with a crescendo to the entries of the first theme, and how these crescendos are never allowed to rise above a certain pitch of intensity until they culminate in the final massive climax. By far the most stirring entry of the subject is the final one in the bass.

Before referring to the composers of fugues who flourished between Sweelinck and Frescobaldi and Bach, it will be advisable to analyse the form in detail so that all technicalities may be understood.

You have probably noticed that in a fugue, although each part makes its entry with the theme, the key and consequently the pitch of the entries varies. Keen observers may have solved the plan or convention of these alterations, which is briefly as follows. The part which first states the subject naturally does so in the tonic, or key in which the piece is to begin and finish. The next part to enter has the theme transposed either a fifth higher or a fourth lower into the dominant key, that is, the key with one sharp more or one flat less and most closely related to the original key. If the subject changes key during

its course, then that which is in the tonic in the original statement goes into the dominant for the second entrant, and that
which is in the dominant in the subject goes back into the
tonic. The third entry is like the first, and the fourth like the
second. This originated in the motet. It was due to the com-
passes of the different types of the human voice. Sopranos
and tenors got the theme at a higher pitch than altos and
basses. The ecclesiastical modes were arbitrary limitations
imposed by church musicians, not a selection of sounds related
to one another acoustically like modern scales. All music was
originally entirely melodic. When the idea of two or more
parts singing different sounds occurred to composers—the
dawn of harmony—a difficulty at once presented itself. How
could the higher and lower voices all keep to the same mode?
For instance, the Mixolydian mode lies between g' and g":
all tunes in this mode had to keep within these notes and
finish on g', a compass impossible for altos and basses. The
difficulty was overcome by inventing a second set of modes
called 'plagal' modes, which had their final or keynotes in the
middle instead of at the extremes. Thus the plagal version of
the Mixolydian lay between d' and d" with the final g' in the
middle. Then the original or authentic modes divided into a
fifth—tonic to dominant—followed by a fourth—dominant to
tonic—whilst the plagal modes divided into a fourth—dominant to tonic—followed by a fifth—tonic to dominant. This
arbitrary convention forced the composer to adjust his tunes
to a certain extent when they appeared in the plagal mode.
Fourths became fifths and vice versa; phrases or parts of them
which had the compass of a fifth in the authentic mode were
compressed within the compass of a fourth in the plagal. It is
not necessary to go into more detail than this. One or two
examples from Bach's Forty-eight will show the type of alteration, for instance, E flat, Book I (4); E flat, Book II (4). The
main thing for us to appreciate is that subjects altered according to these conventions seem in some mysterious way to give
an answer to a question asked by the original statement of the
theme. Thus the version of the subject sung by the second and
fourth parts in order of entry has become known as the 'answer'.
It is wonderful how an arbitrary and, to our minds, rather
stupid convention by its very limitations often leads to a freshness and added beauty which, without the convention, might

have been missed. Fashion in dress is an example. Elizabethan hoops and ruffs and Caroline and Georgian wigs and women's highly dressed coiffures must have been uncomfortable and inconvenient. But to us in later times they have a romantic charm.

Composers often broke rules without destroying the beauty which might be attributed to them. Thus Bach sometimes makes an answer to a fugue subject which, although it invariably has the true effect of an answer, is not written in strict accordance with the rules that have been stated; for instance, the G sharp minor, Book I (18).

Subjects are of three distinct types. First, long complete phrases, usually of such beauty and interest that to hear each entry of them without added contrapuntal device is sufficient, as, for example, the E minor fugue in Book II, No. 10, and the great G minor organ fugue. Such a subject was called an 'Andamento' (Italian, 'gait' or 'movement'). Second, the ordinary fairly short subject such as those already instanced. This was termed a 'Soggetto'. Third, one rhythmic figure only, which was used in a few fugues. This was called an 'Attacco' (Italian, 'attachment'). Examples may be found in the C sharp major, No. 3 in Book II, and the D major, No. 5 in Book II.

When the second part to enter sings the answer, the first part sings the countersubject[1]—a new theme in rhythmic contrast to the subject itself. The word counterpoint, 'against a point', really implies a counter-theme. The word point was the term applied to a number of voices entering successively with the same theme. Against, or counter to this, was placed some other tune. The subject and countersubject are like husband and wife: they should blend and yet contrast with each other. It was Bach who gave the countersubject its importance, and a position secondary only to the subject itself. When all the parts have made their entry with subject and answer the exposition—the giving out of the text several times—is completed. Naturally at this point there must be some relief and contrast. This is afforded by an episode. Episodes do not contain either subject or countersubject in their entirety, but they may be constructed from some portion of them. In exceptional cases they are of new material, but in the same mood and pulse as the subject. In most cases they are the less strenuous

[1] The F sharp minor and the St. Anne are exceptions.

E

portions of the fugue. But, after allowing the tension to slacken, they often begin a crescendo which leads to the next entry of the subject, but now in a fresh key. This middle section of a fugue has the same function as the third phrase of a melody or the development section in sonata form: excitement and interest are enhanced by change from key to key, episodes alternate with entries of the subject in all parts, until at last there is a return to the principal key in which a final triumphal entry of the theme is made, and a coda brings the piece to a conclusion.

The form and style of the longer concerto and sonata movements discussed at the end of Chapter III can now be better understood, for they show the influence of the fugue as well as the ancient binary form. Seeing what a dominant part the fugue played in the musical life of the seventeenth and eighteenth centuries it was to be expected that composers would not entirely eliminate it from their minds even when writing in other forms. The composers were nearly always organists, and counterpoint was in their blood. The character of the themes has already been referred to. The episodes, although more often consisting of new matter, still resemble fugal episodes in as much as they are of less intensity than what precedes and follows, and often lead through a crescendo to a re-entry of the subject in a new key. The plan of stating the theme in various keys finishing with the tonic was common to both forms.

The composers of fugues who flourished between the first quarter of the seventeenth century and the time of Bach were German organists. The solemn organ and the intricacies of fugal movements appealed to the serious Teutonic temperament. The earlier ones were South Germans and wrote in the smooth Italian style for the Roman Church. The later ones were North German Protestants. Their music has a stronger and more rugged flavour. What we are chiefly concerned with is what they accomplished in advancing the art of fugal writing.

Johann Jacob Froberger (b. early seventeenth century, d. 1667) was a pupil of Frescobaldi. His Capriccio[1] in G shows him to be a faithful disciple of his master and yet able to perceive his shortcomings, for it is a string of short fugues like

---

[1] Seventeenth-century titles do not always offer an explanation of the form. Practically any combination of movements might be termed a 'Sonata' in those days.

the work by Frescobaldi already discussed. Froberger unifies his Capriccio by using the same theme for each of the five fughettas. He metamorphoses its rhythm, not so completely as to destroy its identity, but enough to give variety and accumulate interest. Continuity is achieved by better joins than in Frescobaldi. There is only one definite stop between the sections—at the end of the fourth. The others are joined either by allowing the new one to begin on the last note of the cadence of the previous one, or by using only a half-cadence to end a section. The amount of movement increases as the work progresses.

Johann Kaspar Kerll (1627–93) is chiefly remembered because Handel used one of his fugues in his oratorio *Israel in Egypt*, setting it to the words 'Egypt was glad when they departed'. It is quite a noteworthy fugue as a piece of craftsmanship, and has a little emotional feeling as well, obtained through a cumulative building up of the interest. It is noteworthy because the answer is an inversion of the subject and because a stretto is made before the completion of the exposition. About two-fifths of the fugue is concerned with ever closer strettos on the main theme. Then, after a cadence, a new counter-theme makes its appearance with slightly quicker movement. This is answered by inversion and immediately combined with the first theme. The middle section is a maze of strettos on both versions of subject and countersubject. The coda is entirely concerned with the countersubject. His Canzona in C is also the work of a sound craftsman and one who was evidently anxious to break fresh ground. It has a florid countersubject. The order of entry is subject, answer, answer, subject, as in No. 1, Book I, of the Forty-eight. At one-third of its length it comes to rest on the dominant chord with a repeat indicated: an attempt to unite ancient binary form with fugue. The second part begins with a short exposition on two fresh counter-subjects. These are afterwards combined with the theme and the original florid countersubject. A stretto on the first subject together with the florid countersubject, and one final entry of the subject in the bass, bring this interesting fugue to a satisfying conclusion.

Johann Pachelbel (1653–1706) was a pupil of Kerll in Vienna and spent the earlier part of his career amid the softer influences of South Germany. In the end he returned to Nüremberg, where he was born, and finished his life as a North German Protestant organist. He wrote in his earlier period many fugues which have a silky, smoothly-flowing counterpoint, but do not show that Pachelbel had foreseen the lines on which the great fugues of Bach were to be built. He uses countersubjects and then forsakes them, just as Sweelinck did so many years before: he introduces extraneous material, especially in his codas, that has no affinity with what has preceded it. He was indeed a forerunner of Bach, but not in fugue: he is better remembered for his choral preludes, of which more will be said later on. This is in a lesser sense true of *Dietrich Buxtehude* (1637–1707), probably the greatest of all the North German School. His fugues, like those of his contemporaries and predecessors, despite their strength and dignity cannot keep going for very long because they are devoid of episodes. The texts are constantly repeated but no subsidiary ideas emanate from them. The constant recurrence of the subject soon becomes monotonous no matter how many different counterpoints appear with it. This accounts for the string of little fugues, some of them with the same subject metamorphosed, and others with new subjects. Buxtehude's set of fugues from his Praeludium und Fuge in G minor are an example. The first one has no countersubject and finishes with a perfect cadence in the tonic and a long chord of G minor. The second begins again in G minor on a new subject. It would have been far better to dovetail the final bar of number one on to the first bar of number two, as Froberger did. The second fugue has no countersubject, but it does end with a half-cadence on the dominant. The third and last has a florid countersubject. The fugues in his Praeludium und Fuge in E minor are much in the same style but are more interesting harmonically and contrapuntally. The first stops short on the tonic chord, as in the G minor, but a brief and brilliant cadenza is inserted between the second and the third.

It has often been said that Bach owed much to these men. No doubt he learned counterpoint from them, and acquired an even greater facility than theirs in the use of the various devices. But there are four outstanding features in the fugues of Bach which are not to be found in the works of the North German School of organist composers. In order of increasing importance they are as follows:

He saw that to use a countersubject throughout a fugue, or even to introduce it in the course of a fugue, so long as it continues to have a prominent place in the structure to the end, gives a double interest, and provides more material to work upon.

His economy, that is, his amazing power of making use of every tiny bit of his original material, binds his structure into one indivisible whole. Every single note contributes to the coherence and unity of the work.

He discovered that the episode could lengthen and broaden out the form and avoid monotony, and his great imagination helped him to write episodes, not so long that his hearers would forget the subject, but long enough to whet their appetites for it when it reappears.

Finally, and most important of all, his technique was so subconscious that his mind could dwell undistracted on the main object of all music—the expression of human feeling. His fugues are amazing in the variety of their emotions.

The examples given below to illustrate these points are all taken from the Forty-eight and the well-known organ fugues.

Countersubjects.

Fugues in which the countersubject has equal, or nearly equal, importance with the subject:

The Forty-eight.

I. 2. Here it appears at every entry of the theme, and all the episodes are constructed from it, so that some form of it is found in every bar except the first two and the last three.

I. 3. Here also the wife accompanies her husband at all his public appearances, and all the episodes originate from her.

I. 12. There are three countersubjects to this fugue. All of them appear in the exposition.

I. 21. This fugue has two countersubjects, both of which appear in the exposition. It is the invertible counterpoint which supplies the interest in this type of fugue; the three themes are repeated in various keys, but always in different parts.

II. 1. The countersubject appears in all entries except the first and last.

II. 4. The countersubject does not enter until the twentieth bar. After that it takes precedence over the subject.

II. 6, 16, and 20 all have important countersubjects.

II. 18. This fugue is of the same type as the F sharp minor in Book II already referred to. It has, however, only one countersubject, which appears at bar 61 and is given an exposition to itself. The two themes are mated at bar 97.

The countersubjects of the St. Anne Fugue have already been quoted. The great E minor organ fugue (the 'Wedge')[1] is an excellent example of what may be done with a countersubject. The last bar forms a cadence figure which marks the close of many of the divisions, as was customary in the dance-forms of the Suites.[2]

Economy.

There is not a fugue amongst the Forty-eight which does not exemplify economy, but perhaps the most amazing example of making much out of little is found in II. 3. The whole of it is built up from the tiny theme (attacco) a bar and a half in length, for even the figure first heard at bar 8 owes its origin to the first four notes of the theme. It is this genius for making the utmost use of material which binds the fugues of Bach into one indissoluble whole. It would lead to monotony were it not that his imagination invented so many different ways of using any figure or theme. The effect on the hearer is a subconscious one, for unless the fugues are carefully scanned the economy is not evident.

Episodes.

The longest episodes are to be found in the great organ fugues, although some of the Forty-eight are very nearly half subject entries and half episode. The organ fugues were, however, designed on a much bigger scale. No one prior to Bach had written long fugal movements really successfully. It was his episodes which enabled him to do this without the danger of the monotony so easily brought about by a continual reiteration of the theme and without pulling up and starting afresh. Examples of these long episodes may be found in nearly all the great organ fugues. Here are a few. The G major, bars 38–52; the G minor (following the Fantasia), bars 82–93; the A minor (six-eight time), bars 31–43, 83–95, 101–12, 119–30; the B

[1] Called 'The Wedge' from the shape of the subject.   [2] See p. 51.

minor, bars 50–58. The great E minor, already referred to, has a form all to itself. It is the union of the toccata with the fugue form. A normal exposition is followed by three further entries of the subject. The middle section of the fugue consists of episodes of new material in the form of toccata-like rushes of semiquavers leading with crescendos of intensity to entries of the first two bars of the theme. There are no less than seven episodes and entries in this section. The sixth returns to the stately quaver movement of the opening. The seventh cleverly dovetails into a complete recapitulation—note for note—of the opening section, both exposition and further entries. This fugue thus has a kinship not only with the toccata but with the longer movements of the concertos and sonatas. The pre-Bach composers also included bravura passages in their fugues, but most of them altered the pace of the beat at these points. A beat of the same pace throughout a movement gives it unity and continuity. Bach realized this in the E minor Fugue.

Variety of emotion.

It has already been shown that as each of the great musical periods reached its zenith the compositions became more human and expressive. The fugues of Bach were the apotheosis of counterpoint, and by far the most human. In the Forty-eight there are examples of the deepest feeling, so serious that they seem to bear out the statement that music begins where words fail. Such are the E flat minor (I. 8), the F minor (I. 12), the B flat minor (I. 22), and the great B minor Fugue for the organ. At the other end of the emotional gamut are light-hearted, carefree fugues like the C sharp major (I. 3), the E flat major (I. 7), the F sharp major (I. 13), the G major (I. 15), the B flat major (I. 21), the F major (II. 11), the great D major for the organ, and the two fughettas forming the two halves of some of the Gigues in the French and English Suites. (These are notable for combining fugue with a dance in binary form.) Between these extremes practically every mood can be found: gentle, tender fugues (F sharp major, I. 13), placid fugues (F major, I. 11), stern fugues of relentless energy (A minor, I. 20), dramatic fugues (A minor, II. 20).

Hitherto we have only discussed fugue because that is the greatest form of contrapuntal music. Those who have thoroughly imbibed what has been said should have no difficulty in comprehending and recognizing any fugato sections in other works.

One more essentially contrapuntal form of instrumental music must be mentioned here, the Choral Prelude (*Choralvorspiel*). It originated in the German Lutheran Church. Luther appreciated to the full the spiritual value of hymnody. He, with the help of contemporary musicians, was the inspiration behind the publication of numerous hymn books from the year 1524 onwards. The tunes or chorals in these books were all excellent for their purpose. Some of them were adapted either from plainsong melodies or from medieval tunes in use in the Roman Church. Some were secular folk-songs, and others were original compositions by Luther and his musical colleagues. So good was the choice of these men and so full of inspiration were their own compositions that these tunes became an essential part of the worship of the Church and have retained their life and freshness to this day. At a time when Church services were often three times as long as those we are accustomed to, it is not surprising that the organist, instead of merely playing over the tune before the hymn was sung, played a prelude founded on the tune. Luther himself advocated the adornment of these simple tunes. He says: 'When natural music is heightened and polished by art, there man first beholds . . . the great and perfect wisdom of God in his marvellous work of music, in which this is most singular and indeed astonishing, that one man sings a simple tune . . . together with which three, four, or five voices also sing, which as it were play and skip delightedly round this simple tune, and wonderfully grace and adorn it.[1]

Some of these choral preludes were written before the end of the sixteenth century. The plan most frequently adopted was to write a point of imitation founded on each successive line of the tune and then introduce the actual tune in a prominent part—usually the uppermost or the bass—often in notes of longer length than the imitations which continued alongside the tune. The imitations contained the contrapuntal devices of diminution and inversion, the tune supplying the augmentation. This form of *Choralvorspiel* was used very often by Bach himself. It no doubt originated in the vocal Motets and Masses, the choral taking the place of the canto fermo so often found

[1] Schweitzer, *J. S. Bach* (Breitkopf and Härtel), Vol. i, p. 29.

in the Mass. Its development follows the lines of the fugue:
the earliest efforts do not seem to aim at suggesting the mood
of the hymn. The texture is often more vocal than instrumental. Such is the Vorspiel, *Vater unser im Himmelriech*, by Samuel
Scheidt (1587–1654) quoted by Parry in the *Oxford History of
Music*.[1] Scheidt also practised another form which was adopted
by Bach. Instead of the lines of the choral supplying the
material for imitation a short original theme was invented
which was used throughout against the canto fermo of the
choral. There is a fine example of this form by Franz Tunder
(1614–67), *Jesus Christus, unser Heiland*. The first three verses
of the hymn are set separately. The first is an elaborate contrapuntal setting in five parts, the choral in the first bass. Verse
two is quiet, and has a new counter-theme not related to the
tune. Verse three is a mighty effort. The tune thunders out in
the bass. The counter-theme is so remarkable that the beginning is worth quoting:

63

Tunder was Buxtehude's predecessor as organist of the Marien-
kirche at Lübeck. He wrote many cantatas founded on chorals.
Bach must have been largely influenced by him. *Jesus Christus*
is a communion hymn, but the music, fine as it is, seems to have
no reference to it.

Pachelbel was among the first to make the choral prelude
reflect the spirit of the hymn. All his preludes seem to do this

[1] Vol. iii, p. 113.

in a general way, and at any rate one of them, *Vom Himmel
hoch*, is even more intimately expressive. The hymn is for
Christmas and the verse in Pachelbel's mind is the thirteenth:

> Ah dearest Jesus, Holy Child,
> Make Thee a bed, soft, undefiled,
> Within my heart, that it may be
> A quiet chamber kept for Thee.

The tune is in the bass. The two upper parts sing the most
delicate and fanciful pastoral which reproduces the quiet re-
flective tenderness of the hymn-stanza quite wonderfully.

Buxtehude's brilliance as a performer shows itself in his
choral preludes. He loved to decorate the tune with embellishments of all sorts and to write bravura passages above it.

Bach learned from these men how to write all three types of
prelude, those with imitations founded on the choral, those
with original counter-themes, and those with decorated chorals.
Being very spiritually-minded and a wonderful craftsman he
used his technique to express the deep feelings which the hymns
created in his own soul. This inspiration, which came from
his religion and from the poems, enabled him to invent counter-
themes and decorative passages which get very close indeed to
the spirit of the hymn. He used the form of the choral prelude
in his cantatas as well as in his organ pieces. The most popular
of all his works founded on a choral, 'Jesu, joy of man's
desiring', comes from a cantata. The same basic idea is found
in both cantata movements and organ preludes—prelude,
phrases of the choral separated by interludes, and often a
postlude to conclude with.

The idea of making the counter-themes suggest the text seems
first to have occurred to Bach when he wrote the *Little Organ
Book* during his sojourn at Cöthen (1717–23). This is a collection of short choral preludes 'wherein instruction is given to
the beginning organist to work out a choral in every style'.
Let us look at one of these, *Ach wie nichtig, ach wie flüchtig*.
The verse of the hymn is as follows:

> O how fleeting,
> O how fading
> Is our earthly being!
> 'Tis a mist in wintry weather,
> Gathered in an hour together,
> And as soon dispersed in ether.

To illustrate this Bach writes scales ascending and descending, like dissolving and changing clouds, or shadows flitting up and down a wall. In Cantata No. 26 he amplifies this idea into a long movement. There is a prelude for orchestra, then the chorus enters, the sopranos having the choral, whilst the three lower parts imitate in diminution, their lightly spoken quavers conjuring up in the listener's emotions the uncertainty of life. The prelude, interludes, and postlude are all constructed from the scale passages to be found in the organ prelude, crossing and recrossing each other.

Bach wrote upwards of a hundred Choral Preludes. It is impossible to select from these a few which will show all his methods and all his depth of feeling. But at any rate there is one which all music lovers should know, *Schmücke dich, O liebe Seele*. Schumann, writing to Mendelssohn, who had played the prelude to him, says: 'Round the *cantus firmus* hung garlands of leaves, and it is full of such beatitude that you yourself confessed to me that if life were to deprive you of hope and faith, this one choral would bring it all back again to you.[1] The hymn begins thus:

> Soul, array thyself with gladness,
> Leave the gloomy caves of sadness;
> Come from doubt and dusk terrestrial,
> Gleam with radiant light celestial.

It seems to be the very first word *schmücke*, to adorn, to embellish, which Bach seeks to illustrate. The way he does it can be seen from the quotations given below.

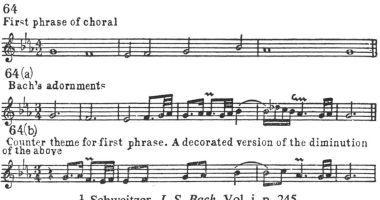

64
First phrase of choral

64 (a)
Bach's adornments

64(b)
Counter theme for first phrase. A decorated version of the diminution of the above

---

[1] Schweitzer, *J. S. Bach*, Vol. i, p. 245.

Thus it will be seen that even the counter-themes are embellished.

Another extraordinary example is the conclusion of the final variation on *Vom Himmel hoch da komm ich her* ('From heaven above to earth I come'), a Christmas hymn. This is a set of five variations in the form of canons either on a counter-theme against the choral in long notes, or on some form of the canto fermo. They were perhaps written more as a *tour de force* than as a direct expression of the hymn. Nevertheless there is a deal of Christmas joy in them. The example is quoted to show Bach's amazing contrapuntal facility. When played, this cadence sounds like a joyous and triumphant ending, as was intended: art conceals art so much that the hearer would never dream that all four lines of the choral are here combined in pure six-part counterpoint.

One more example may be cited, *Wenn wir in höchsten Nöthen sein* ('When we are in deepest need'). The story goes that Bach dictated this to his son-in-law on his death-bed, and altered the title to *Von deinen Thron tret' ich* ('I come before thy throne'), another hymn often sung to this tune. Bach was never afraid of death: all his music on the subject bespeaks a strong faith. This prelude, though very serious, is not sad, except in the last two bars. The counterpoint is just as wonderful as ever. The accompanying parts are engaged the whole time with the diminution and inverted diminution of the various phrases of the choral, yet all flow along in undisturbed serenity. The tune itself is decorated only very slightly in the first phrase. Thus, as his end approached, Bach chose the form of his much-loved *Choralvorspiel* as the medium for his last message.

Counterpoint makes its appearance here and there in practically all the various pieces of instrumental music from the birth of this branch of the art in the late sixteenth right down to the closing years of the eighteenth century. It reached its zenith in Bach. He explored and exploited it in countless different ways. Many fugues and choral preludes have been written by well-known composers since his time, some of them very fine ones. Haydn, Mozart, Beethoven, Mendelssohn, Schumann, and Brahms have all contributed splendid fugues to the repertory, but they contain little that cannot be found in Bach, except that Mozart and Beethoven dovetailed fugue and sonata form successfully. But after Bach's time counterpoint fell into desuetude, and sonata form with its satellites took its place as the most important form.

V

SONATA FORM AND RONDO FORM

No one has ever invented a truly accurate and informative name for sonata form. It has also been termed 'first movement form', because most first movements of sonatas, symphonies, and chamber music have been written in it since the last half of the eighteenth century. But other forms are also used in these works, and therefore the term 'sonata form' is inaccurate; nor are all first movements in this form, which knocks out the description of it as 'first movement form'. It has been called 'binary form' owing to the fact that, like the earlier two-part form described in Chapter III, it comes to a halt in the key of the dominant, or relative major, at the end of the exposition, and starts again and continues without any other hold-up of importance to the end. It has also been classified as 'ternary form', for its second half is divided into two easily recognized sections, the development, or free fantasia, and the recapitulation.

It has already been shown that the form of many ancient melodies contains the essence of it: the statement of a phrase finishing in the tonic followed by another ending in the dominant, or relative major, followed again by an excursion to a key further removed, and ending with a phrase which brings the music back home to the tonic, which phrase is often a repetition of the first.

It has also been shown that even in the late sixteenth century each half of the dance forms was made to finish with the same cadence-figure. Later this became a coda or closing group to round off and give unity to the two halves of the composition.

Sonata form has also a close relationship with the aria form of the operas and oratorios of the eighteenth century, for they had three sections, and the last was a repetition of the first.

In the previous chapter the apotheosis of counterpoint in J. S. Bach and the tendency which followed to try for contrast between consecutive rhythmic groups rather than between intricately weaving parts were mentioned. The crystallizing of the sonata form movement, therefore, gradually evolved partly through a development of the old binary or two-part dance form, and partly through the swing over from counterpoint to melody and harmony in contrasted rhythmic groups.

The actual form, as adhered to fairly strictly by the earliest writers, is as follows. The first subject opens, as a rule, though in some cases there is a slow introduction which may or may not be referred to again in the course of the movement. The subject is always rhythmically arresting, or at all events has something about it melodically which makes it easy to remember, for the enjoyment and appreciation of the form depends on memory. You cannot tell when the composer throws new light on his subjects in the development section if you cannot remember the tunes. He must help you by making it easy for you to keep them in mind: you must help him by putting all other thoughts out of your head and concentrating entirely on the music. A full cadence in the tonic key ends the first subject. A bridge or intermezzo leads from the tonic to the dominant, or to the relative major if the sonata is in a minor key. It does not always lead straight to the dominant or relative major, but often to the key north of them. If the key used in the cadence which brings a section to an end is used to start the next section the effect is sometimes lame; it sounds like the end of one piece and the beginning of a fresh one. By moving into the key on the north side the composer persuades us that something of importance is coming. Haydn and Mozart generally heralded their themes and marked the various sections of the form by very definite cadences, sometimes insisted on by repetition, as if to say to the audience: 'Now sit up and take notice, something important is coming.' The cadences themselves are often of the most ordinary and commonplace type. We know that audiences in those days were casual and badly behaved. They applauded in the middle of the movement if anything took their fancy, and even hissed and booed if they disliked something. Sonata form was young at that time; subtleties would have been incomprehensible. We shall see later that it was Beethoven who found out how to prepare our feelings gradually for his lovely tunes. The exposition is rounded off by a codetta, or closing group, ending in the key of the second subject, as was the case in the old binary form. The exposition is repeated. Then follows the development or free section. The composer is at liberty to develop any or all of the four sets of themes in the exposition, and to modulate to any key he pleases so long as he gives his hearers some excitement and adventure, and an appetite for the reprise. In this last section all the material of the exposition is repeated, but all of it is now in the tonic key. After the closing group there is sometimes a short coda. It is felt that to end the movement with exactly the same material as that which ends the exposition is rather an anti-climax, for it throws the music back to the emotional state existing at that point. Here you have a short summary of the greatest of all musical forms in which Haydn, Mozart, Beethoven, and Brahms wrote movements for their solo sonatas, chamber music, concertos, and symphonies, many of which, especially those of Beethoven, have plumbed the very depths of human feeling.

The suitability of the form for great music can be explained. In the first place it gives opportunity for the inclusion of far more thematic material than the previous forms. Not only are there four distinct and contrasted themes in the exposition (first subject, bridge theme, second subject, and closing group) but each of the four may have more than one rhythmic group. Even in such an early Beethoven work as the Pianoforte Sonata in E flat, op. 7, there are four different rhythmic interests and contrasts in the first subject, one in the bridge, four in the second subject, and two in the closing group—a total of eleven. It is obvious that very short movements have not the same depth of inspiration as long ones, nor have they the same chance of working upon the emotions of the hearer. It is also obvious that a long movement needs more subject material than a short one. It is also palpable that the character of themes is enhanced by contrast. A noble first subject, like that of the 'Eroica' Symphony for instance, will sound more noble when heard alongside the gentle, appealing second theme than it would if an attempt were made to give the whole movement a lofty austerity. The development section gives composers a bigger chance to allow their imagination free play than any other form.

Let us now examine an early work employing sonata form, and then follow its gradual development. It is said that J. S. Bach's son, Carl Philipp Emanuel (1714–88), was its inventor. At any rate he settled the formula just explained. Later com-

posers saw its possibilities and developed the idea of contrasted rhythms, and Haydn was one of the first to acknowledge
his indebtedness to C. P. E. Bach. In the movement that we
are to consider, the first movement of C. P. E. Bach's Sonata
in D, there is a fairly well-defined second subject which appears
in the tonic at the recapitulation. But it is not in complete
contrast to the first theme, in fact it is accompanied by the
same rhythmic figure—the heroine is still very much like the
hero. One can still feel the influence of the old binary form in
the exposition, where one rhythm pervades the whole. The
second half begins with the theme in the dominant, just as in
the conventional binary form. But the modulations which
follow are quite bold; the music, beginning in E, goes through
G sharp minor and C sharp minor: a good choice seeing that
the exposition and recapitulation are all in major keys. Reference is made to all the principal thematic material of the exposition, and there is a little new stuff which, however, fits in
quite well. The return to the first theme suggests that Bach
was beginning to realize the importance of this point in sonata
form, but had not the experience to turn it to the best advantage. One very noteworthy feature occurs at the end of the
closing group: a coda is added. It has no reference to what has
gone before, but it links up the first movement with the slow
movement which follows. This was indeed prophetic, for many
composers have realized that once you bring a movement to
an obvious finish, you must begin whatever follows at zero as
far as the interest of the audience is concerned. On the other
hand, no one is capable of sustained concentration and attention beyond a certain length of time. The relaxation and
silence between the movements of a great work is a necessary
relief. The composer must settle the matter and decide whether
he can hold his audience for two or more movements without
a pause. In his Fifth Symphony Beethoven leads his Scherzo
into the last movement without a break. Attempts have been
made within our own memory to write one-movement works
on a grand scale. They are not really one-movement works,
for slow movements and quick ones are all included without
any definite stop. As a rule, most of us prefer the relaxations.

C. P. E. Bach was a virtuoso of European reputation on
the clavier, and anticipated men like Liszt in the new and
brilliant effects he invented for his instrument. Although he

F

was the son of the greatest contrapuntist of all time, he
despised counterpoint. He told our English historian, Burney,
that canons were dry and despicable pieces of pedantry that
anyone might compose who would give his time to them.
This remark shows how the pendulum was swinging over. He
was a very voluminous composer: he wrote ninety clavier
sonatas and no fewer than six hundred odd other works. He
was writing sonatas as early as 1742, during his father's life-
time. Yet he is practically forgotten, whilst his father's counterpoint is more loved and appreciated than ever. He was a
pioneer and an experimenter, but the new fashion in music was
so popular that he was carried away on its tide, and failed to
see the greatness of the older counterpoint.

The difficulty in writing sonata form successfully is not lack
of variety but lack of unity. The older forms had rhythms
and figures which persisted throughout a movement, but the
new form was built on the opposite principle—the contrast of
rhythms. The only thing to unify the form, to hold it together
and keep it moving along, was the pulse or beat. Therefore,
whether a theme was chiefly in short notes or long ones, the
pace of the beats remained constant. Having thrown over
counterpoint where if one part was in long notes another
could keep things alive and moving, composers hunted about
for something to replace this effect of constant movement.
To use block chords might be sufficient here and there, but
not all through. A musician named Alberti (1710–40) discovered the idea of playing the notes of a chord separately
instead of simultaneously, but with the notes of each chord
taken in the same succession in each group. On the top of
this rippling accompaniment a composer wrote his melodies.
This became known as the 'Alberti Bass'. Examples of this,
in one form or another, may be found in practically every
piano sonata of Haydn and Mozart. Alberti himself used it
continuously in some of his sonatas. I suppose it must be the
most overworked drudge in music of all time. The commonest
form is 1,3,2,3; 1 being the lowest note of a three-note chord.

66

I have not worked out all the permutations one could get from a three-note chord with one note repeated to keep up a movement of four notes to the beat. With three notes to the beat there are six different changes, but the one I have given was oftenest used, probably because it begins with the bass-note—he bass governs the harmonic progression—and because it contains no repeated notes, which were difficult at a rapid pace on harpsichords and clavichords.

As one would expect, composers, to begin with, were quite satisfied with their new ideas for their own sake. As we found in fugue, but in a rather different way, they were interested in the ideas themselves—rhythmic contrast, the invention of shapely and beautiful themes, and their development—but not so much in the emotional effect these would make on the hearer. Moreover, the early writers of sonata form lived in a formal and conventional age when a child addressed his father as 'Sir' and his mother as 'Madam'. Nearly all his life Haydn was the chief musician of wealthy aristocrats, and so was Mozart for a time. They wore liveries and sat below the salt. This saved them from the temptation of writing down to the level of a popular audience and gave them plenty of time to compose, but it made them subservient, formal, and deferential to a certain extent. Walter Pater says that there are two stimuli behind an artist, the desire to create beauty and the impulse to express emotion. In the greatest geniuses these two are balanced. In lesser men they are not. Those whose sole motive is to create beauty apart from feeling develop into mere craftsmen, while the man who is out to express through his art the feelings of his heart may, if he has not learned his craft, which will show him what is beautiful and what is not, create ugliness which might excite emotion, but could not permanently endure, being built on the sand. The terms 'classical' and 'romantic' have come into use through these two great influences, but applied to music they are not accurate descriptions of anything truly inspired. Both factors are at work in the souls of all the greatest men, though for reasons already given—the characteristics of the age, the nature of their employment, and the newness of the form—the works of Haydn and Mozart lean towards the formal, or classical, side. Beethoven's opus 1 was published in 1795, six years after the French Revolution. Equality and the brotherhood of man were burning subjects in his day. Instead of being a liveried servant, like a superior butler, he was invited by the aristocracy to make music for them. This emancipation levelled up the two impulses in him. He used form to help his expression.

Let us now look into the works of these three great geniuses and learn how each of them used sonata form. Haydn, 1732–1809, is one of the best-loved musicians. His music brims over with the joy of life. Even if he adopts a minor key he always seems glad to quit it as soon as may be. He must have lived a sheltered, quiet, and happy life, for his patron, Prince Esterhazy, allowed him the freedom due to an old and valued servant. He was with him from 1761 to 1790. In the latter year he visited London, and for the first time in his life was lionized. A second visit took place in 1794. Mozart, on the other hand, was touring and playing before large and critical audiences at the age of six. Mozart was a man of the world before he was in his 'teens. Haydn never became a man of the world. He was a simple peasant and spoke a broad Austrian dialect to the day of his death. His music abounds in tunes which have a strong affinity with the folk-songs of his native Croatia. There is a childlike—not childish—naïveté about his music which is not to be found in the polished, calculated perfection of Mozart's. Haydn was thirty when Mozart began his musical life, and his influence upon him was great. When Mozart died in 1791 Haydn still had eighteen years left to him, and in these he did his greatest work. Mozart was probably the most naturally gifted of all the great musicians. So prolific was he that in his short life of thirty-five years he wrote over six hundred works. Schubert and Mozart overflowed with melody of the greatest beauty. It poured from them in a never-ending stream. Haydn began to write sonata form in the transitional state in which C. P. E. Bach left it: the second subject often scarcely distinguishable from the first, the other two components—bridge and closing group—mere bravura. Even Mozart's early works show these characteristics, but it was not long before Mozart saw the advantage of contrast of themes and the necessity for making the subsidiary sections something more than mere flourishes. He then began to write intermezzos and codettas of real musical interest. Haydn learnt these things from Mozart and put them into practice in the works he wrote after Mozart's death. Both of them re-

mained formalists to the end. All the great composers have
produced their masterpieces despite the customs, rules, and
limitations of their time. All have profited by the work of their
predecessors.

Mozart never experimented with sonata form. He knew
that his genius and his fertility in melody would supply him
with all he wanted within the limits of the conventions. Haydn
did experiment and progress, chiefly in harmony and in the
development section of the form. Neither of them used form
as a means of expressing emotions as Beethoven did. Their
feelings came through despite the formalism. This was characteristic of the eighteenth century. Let me quote from a transla-
tion by Henry Newbolt of a French poem. It is called 'Gavotte'
and gives us a vivid picture of an eighteenth-century dance in
a few well-chosen words. The italics are mine:

> Courage advancing, strong and tender,
>   Grace untender fanning desire.
> Suppliant conquest, proud surrender,
>   *Courtesy cold of hearts on fire.*
> Willowy, billowy, now they're bending,
>   Low they're bending down-dropped eyes.
> Stately measures, stately ending,
>   Music sobbing and a dream that dies.

Haydn's happiest medium was the string quartet. He wrote
eighty-three, and his vast experience of this combination
helped him enormously, making his touch sure and his judge-
ment safe. Four artists can get the utmost from the material;
playing on the most expressive of all instruments, with only
one line of the score allotted to each, they have the advantage
over the solo pianist. Yet the material given to them must be
of the best, for they cannot command colour to distract and
cover weaknesses, as in the case of an orchestra.

Let us examine a first movement from a Haydn sonata: the
English Sonata in C, so-called because it was written during
a visit to this country. It was dedicated to his friend Mrs.
Bartolozzi. The thematic material is slight. The first subject
provides nearly the whole of it. The second subject has a very
similar rhythm to that of the bridge passage, so that it presents
no contrast at all. The rest is either trimmings to accompany
references to the first subject, or trimmings alone. The de-

velopment is more notable for its modulation to far-off keys rather than for any new light it throws on the first subject. It begins with a statement of the first subject, not in the dominant major, but in the dominant minor, in the left hand with trimmings in the right hand. The music then passes through F major and minor and such distant and unrelated keys as E flat, A flat, C minor, A minor, and D minor. It finally comes to an expectant pause on the dominant seventh of C. The recapitulation is normal and there is no coda. Notice that the two subsidiary sections, the bridge and the closing group, consist mostly of mere ornament.

The next illustration is the first movement of one of Haydn's last quartets, op. 77, no. 2, in F. The exposition is very like that of the sonata. After the first subject, the bridge passage is ornate and somewhat trivial, even though it contains a little invertible counterpoint of a primitive type compared with that of Bach. The second subject is merely the first with a counter-theme on the top of it, and is heralded by a formal cadence of well-worn character. The closing group is a commonplace passage of four bars; its effect is obtained from the loud unison of the strings, not by any innate beauty. The development begins with the theme in the dominant—as was the previous custom—but divided and imitated. Then occurs the passage that makes this movement worth while as an illustration. It is founded on part of the bridge passage, and really does throw new light on it. Beautiful as it is, with its close imitations and daring modulations, its effect depends on harmony, not on the quality of the thematic material, which is conventional. After this there is quite a dramatic moment before the theme enters in E minor, a most unexpected key, then a return is made to the bridge theme, which this time leads us to the usual dominant seventh of the principal key followed by the recapitulation. There is a short coda of five bars, but it only emphasizes the return to the key of the tonic.

As Haydn's happiest medium was the string quartet, so Mozart's was the concerto for the piano. It was he who stabilized the form of the first movement of a concerto. Sonata form is the basis, the differences made by Mozart being calculated to render it more suitable for its purpose. In the aria of opera and oratorio it had been discovered that if the tune is played by the orchestra and repeated by a single voice with light accompaniment a most attractive effect is produced. The sudden cessation of the full-blooded sound of the band and the entry of a lovely voice held people spell-bound. Mozart used this idea in his concertos, and it was similarly employed by subsequent composers—the various sections of the form are first announced by the orchestra and then repeated by the soloist, lightly accompanied. The first *tutti* for orchestra introduces both first and second subjects and ends in the tonic. These are repeated by the soloist and are followed by a short *tutti* corresponding to the codetta, ending in the dominant. The development gives the soloist his second chance. It is succeeded by a compressed recapitulation by orchestra, leading to the further restatement of the themes by the soloist. The final *tutti* leads to a pause on the dominant, near the end, to anticipate the cadenza. This was originally improvised by the soloist, but in later times was either written by the composer or soloist, or by a third person. It is intended not merely to be a *tour de force*, but a means by which the composer can show how the solo instrument can deal with the thematic material of the movement.

Let us now examine the first movement of the Piano Sonata in D (K.576) written in 1789, two years before his death. In it you will notice that by now the effect of rhythmic contrast is exploited to a much greater extent. The two first phrases of the first subject are in direct contrast. The first is bold, loud, and heavy, the second is a ripple of laughter. The two following phrases are in the same contrast. The two ideas are then combined with the heavy theme in the left hand. The first subject ends with a perfect cadence, upon the final chord of which the bridge passage begins. This is quite interesting, and not merely scales and arpeggios. Its first section leads to the dominant as usual, but is interrupted by a marked cadence to introduce a very close canon founded on the first subject. This was quite a novelty. After that there is a little flourish leading to another full stop. Then is heard the delicate, tender little second subject, quite different from all that precedes it, and yet not in any way a clash, and tending to enhance the effect of the rest. Six bars of very ordinary codetta bring the exposition to a close. Immediately we are plunged into the dominant minor (as in Haydn) but by a repetition of the last two bars of the closing group, not by a restatement of the first theme. These two bars play a very important part in the development, so make a mental note of them. After repeating them once the music goes into a distant key—B flat—and a new canon on the first theme appears. This time, instead of a distance of only one quaver before the second part enters, there is a whole bar. This canon is followed by another in G minor at the distance of half a bar with the left hand leading instead of the right. After bold modulations to A minor and B minor, Mozart proceeds to make three separate crescendos founded on the closing-group figure. Each one tempts us to believe that a climax is coming, but it is the fourth that leads triumphantly into the recapitulation. This time he gives us an intermezzo with some more canonical imitation, but leads into the same flourishes just before the second subject. After this, so intrigued is he with his canons that instead of proceeding to the codetta, he inserts a very unexpected modulation to B minor, follows with another canon and then uses some of the material from the intermezzo which he previously omitted. Finally he ends with the codetta exactly as in the exposition. Mozart could write counterpoint second to none except Bach, but he seldom employed it in sonata form. It was melody in which he excelled.

The first movement of the Piano Concerto in A (K.488), written in 1786, presents no complications and is easy to follow. All the themes are in such complete contrast that they can easily be detected whenever they appear. There are five themes in the first orchestral *tutti*. These are repeated in the first solo section with many new decorations and new points of interest as they are shared by soloist and orchestra. Notice the marked cadences which still formally divide the sections. Also observe the introduction of an important new theme. This occurs after the soloist has given out the second subject followed by some decorative passages, and after the orchestra has repeated the bridge theme from which all the orchestral *tutti* are derived. This new theme is played by the strings. It is followed by another bravura passage for the soloist, and a cadence is made in E, the key of the second subject. It is not an obtrusive 'sit-up-and-take-notice' cadence, but a very quiet one, hardly noticeable. It is followed at once by a short development on the new subject, modulating freely. The recapitulation is shortened by playing the themes once, divided between soloist and orchestra, instead of twice, once by the orchestra and once by the soloist. After the second subject there is a long coda. It is founded on the new theme used in the development. The cadenza was written by Mozart. It is most concerned with the various themes and has but few flourishes. The final orchestral *tutti* is constructed from the bridge theme. The movement is an example of balanced form and contrasted themes all blending and helping to make a perfect whole.

When comparing Beethoven with Mozart the word that springs to one's mind is *drama*. My dictionary gives its meaning as follows: 'A poem or composition representing life and action. A series of events invested with the unity and interest of a play.' Mozart used sonata form as the most convenient framework to enclose his perfect melodies and give them every chance by contrast. Beethoven used it in this way also. But even in his earliest essays the drama, human emotion, life, and action, peep out very often. As he progressed this genius for writing music charged with all the deep feelings of mankind gradually pervaded his work more and more. The prim conventions of Mozart's bravura and his formal cadential punctuations were not a musical language for Beethoven. He wanted something more real, more heartfelt, than flourishes, however classically beautiful they might be. It is he who gives not only rhythmic but emotional contrast to his themes. It is he who knows how to prepare our feelings and gradually to allow the music to change from the emotion of one theme and anticipate that of the next. In the very first piano sonata there is a fiery climax at the seventh bar followed by a dramatic pause. There is no formal cadence of any sort. Instead of the usual scale and arpeggio closing group there is a most intense passage: the music surges up from a piano to a fortissimo in seven bars. The return to the first theme is also most dramatic.

Let us begin with a composition typical of Beethoven's earliest style, the Piano Sonata in E flat, op. 7, first movement. It has already been said that there are no less than eleven different rhythmic elements in the exposition. After a calm opening to his second subject he suddenly whips the music up into a frenzy and changes to a remote key—an unheard of thing at this point, where the dominant key should be strictly adhered to. After a few bars in this key he abruptly switches back to the dominant and continues the next section of the second subject. After introducing us in the exposition to all his characters in the play, Beethoven felt that the beginning of the development is where the real drama begins. He used this place in the form over and over again to give us some unexpected thrill. Here he makes a fortissimo statement of the first theme in another unexpected key. He then develops the final closing group theme and gradually builds up quite a tragic climax which is followed by another abrupt modulation and a pathetic reference to the opening bars of the first theme in another totally unexpected key. Finally the development ends in D minor with a rallentando. How shall we get back home safely? One chord is sufficient. It is like a man who imagines he is miles from home on a stormy night and then comes across a signpost which tells him that his destination is close at hand. It is the old trick of the novelist and playwright —persuading us that the hero could never survive his desperate straits, and then relieving our tense feelings by inventing an escape. After the normal recapitulation there is a really typical Beethoven coda. He knew that an audience is quite willing to have its feelings harrowed once more, even when the hero has returned, so long as all turns out happily in the end. And so, instead of the mere emphasis of the tonic key by a few flourishes or oft-repeated cadences, he makes his codas a new adventure. In this movement he starts by once more giving the originally genial first subject another violent and tragic restatement in a foreign key. But very soon the gentle, feminine second subject comes to the rescue and all ends happily.

Our last illustration of sonata form will be the first movement of the 'Waldstein' Sonata in C, op. 53. It contains many characteristic features, and its familiarity will help you to follow the form without trouble. The repeated pianissimo chords of the first subject at once suggest momentous happenings later on. The sudden change to C minor and the pause on the dominant produce the same effect. The theme is repeated with a tremolo instead of the reiterated chords. This enhances the sense of drama to come. We have not long to wait. The music quickly passes into E minor, in which key there is a half-cadence, and the second subject—again unmistakably the heroine—enters in the key of E major. This is indeed a new departure. Instead of the usual dominant we have here a key centre much further removed. Beethoven is very clever at making temporary excursions into distant keys without disturbing the underlying feeling for the original key. He is also a genius at adopting unconventional keys, and yet never loses his way or leaves a sense of vagueness. In this movement there are three distinct sections to the second subject, all in the key of E major. The closing group leads naturally into E minor. Its final phrase is repeated in C, leading to a repeat of the exposition. At the end of this repeat the final section of the closing group is altered so as to lead into F, in which key the development begins with a statement of the first four bars of the first subject. Then follows a very characteristic feature. Beethoven takes two small rhythmic germs from his first theme found in the third and fourth bars:

He draws them closer—they occupy one bar instead of two— thus whipping up the movement and increasing the tension. Even when the music is pianissimo one can feel the increasing excitement, for here he uses only the first germ but changes key rapidly. A long passage founded on the second section of the second subject, still restlessly changing from key to key, lands us on the dominant, G, of the original key. The exciting crescendo on this G is really constructed from the tiny germ (No. 2) heard at the beginning of the development, although this is hardly noticeable. Still it has its effect in strengthening the unity of the movement. The recapitulation has a new feature. There are two dramatic pauses instead of only one, both of them avoiding the dominant of the opening. Three bars of entirely new material switch us back into C and the tremolo version of the first subject succeeds. This time the second subject comes in A. This is even more revolutionary than putting the first version of it into E, for the recapitulation was traditionally all in the original key to establish it. However, in a few bars, Beethoven proceeds through A minor to C, in which key the second subject is repeated. The recapitulation then proceeds normally to the closing group. This is altered so as to finish in D flat. A restatement of the first subject is then made in that key and this begins the long coda. Here he uses the two rhythmic cells already mentioned, but with much more exciting effect, finishing on a dominant seventh. Then follows a reminiscence of the beautiful second subject. The music dies down and slows up to persuade us that all energy and movement are exhausted. Then with a sudden resumption of the tempo the first theme is heard once more surging up from *pp* to *ff* in four bars, and all is over.

Beethoven's codas are usually either dramatic, that is, sudden plunges into further exciting adventures, or reminiscent, where beauties heard previously are recalled. These ideas are also to be found in the novel—the second harrowing of the reader's feelings, and the type of finish wherein the hero recounts his adventures to his children around the fire on winter evenings. They are both examples of the reluctance which the artist and his audience feel in leaving an entrancing subject. Both are loath to quit what has been to them a source of so much pleasure and thrill.

Thus it will be seen that every detail of sonata form was to evolve from a mere rule to a means of conveying feeling, and that the great master who showed the way to this was Beethoven.

Of the other forms used in the various movements of the sonata and its big brother, the symphony, rondo form is the most important, for it, like sonata form, will serve as a framework on which to build a long and important movement. In common with all forms that originated in song and dance it has a very ancient lineage. The French poem, or song, called a *rondeau* or *rondel*, dates back at least to the fourteenth century. It consists of a couplet with which the poem begins and ends, and which is repeated between each stanza. An example is referred to in Chapter I, Purcell's song 'I attempt from love's sickness to fly'. The hymn 'All glory, laud, and honour' is a rondo. The instrumental form commonly known as 'ancient rondo form' follows exactly the same plan: the first subject begins and ends the piece and is repeated between several contrasted portions. A well-known example is Haydn's 'Gypsy Rondo'.[1] Mozart occasionally uses this simple form

---

[1] Piano arrangement from Trio No. 1.

for final movements, as in the Sonata in B flat for piano (K.281), the Sonata in A minor (K.310) and, in an abbreviated form ((*a*) (*b*) (*a*) (*b*) shortened coda), in the well-known 'Rondo alla Turca', the Finale of the Sonata in A (K.331). He also wrote a few slow movements in this form, for instance, the Andante of the Sonata in C (K.545) and the Adagio of the Sonata in B flat (K.570). It is obvious that the principal theme must be particularly attractive seeing that it has to recur so often. Mozart makes his transitional passages leading to the recurrences most affectionate. Both these points are well exemplified in the above-mentioned Adagio and in the slow movement of Beethoven's Sonata in C minor (the 'Pathétique'), op. 13.

For movements on a big scale, however, a variant and improvement on ancient rondo form was evolved, generally known as sonata-rondo. This owed its birth to sonata form, for it has a second subject which appears after the principal theme in the key of the dominant or relative major, and again in the final recapitulation, but this time in the tonic as in sonata form. The formula, therefore, runs like this: (*a*) principal subject, (*b*) second subject (dominant or relative major), repetition of (*a*) in the tonic, (*c*) a middle section in considerable contrast as to rhythm and key, then a recapitulation of (*a*) and (*b*), both in the tonic, followed by a coda wherein are references to either (*a*), (*b*), or (*c*), or all three. The refrain or chorus of a song is stimulating both to performers and listeners. Songs with choruses, therefore, are practically always jolly songs. The rondo is the jolly movement of the sonata for the same reason, and comes last to leave a happy atmosphere at the conclusion of the work. Mozart used several variants of the form. He sometimes makes the middle section (*c*) a development of previous material (Andante from the Sonata in G (K.283), last movement of Sonata in C (K.545)). Occasionally, in the recapitulation after the middle section (*c*), the themes recur in a different order, as in the big-scale rondo in the Sonata in C (K.309), the form of which is as follows: first subject (*a*) in C, intermezzo or bridge leading to the second subject (*b*) in G, transition to (*a*) in C, reference to the rhythm of the third figure in (*b*), which leads to the middle section (*c*) in F. Then follows the whole of (*b*) in the tonic key followed by (*a*) and a coda in which the bridge theme appears again. In the rondo ending the great Fantasia and Sonata in C minor (K.457), the middle section (c) consists of only two phrases. The recapitulation then commences with (b) in the tonic instead of the dominant, and is followed by (a) most movingly broken up into recitative-like utterances. Then comes the coda with an effective reference to (c) and to the interval of the diminished seventh which occurs twice in (a) at its first appearance. Another fine example is the rondo ending the Sonata in D (K.576). Here a similar plan is followed, the first subject coming last in the recapitulation. Instead of a middle section there is a development of the second subject with free modulations. In this section there is another example of the canonical imitation to be found in the first movement already discussed.

Beethoven took comparatively few licences with rondo form. Sometimes he brings the first subject back in the dominant instead of the tonic at its second appearance (Piano Sonatas in F minor, op. 2, no. 1, and the 'Appassionata', op. 57). Sometimes, like Mozart, he prefers to substitute a development section for the contrasted middle section (Sonatas in E flat, op. 27, no. 1, 'allegro vivace', and F minor, op. 57). Sometimes there is a mixture of new material and the development of first or second subjects (Sonata in B flat, op. 22). Perhaps the dramatic element does not enter into the rondos as frequently as in the movements in sonata form, but now and then, even in these carefree movements, there are tense moments when the rhythm is broken and an unexpected modulation is made to some far-off key (Sonata in E flat, op. 7, beginning of the coda; Sonata in D, op. 10, no. 3, middle section and coda; Sonata in F minor, op. 57, end of development; Sonata in F sharp, op. 78, end of the movement).

The slow movements of the sonatas and symphonies are the least conventional in form, especially in Beethoven. The deep feeling expressed, and the slow tempo which does not allow of much repetition lest the movement should become inordinately long, make it advisable to use shorter forms than sonata form or sonata-rondo. Various types of shortened sonata form, therefore, are often used. But there are examples of complete sonata and sonata-rondo in which each member of the form is quite short. Mozart uses full sonata form in the Andante from the Sonata in B flat (K.281), and full rondo in the Adagio from the Sonata in C minor (K.457). Best of all is the long

Andante from the Sonata in F (K.533), in sonata form, with a comparatively long and very interesting development of the first subject and a coda of nine bars. Beethoven uses the complete form in the Adagio con molt' expressivo from the Sonata in B flat, op. 22.

There are two methods of shortening sonata form. The second subject can follow the first without an intermezzo (Adagio of Sonata in F, Mozart (K.280)), or the development can be omitted (Adagio of Sonata in F, Mozart (K.332); Adagio of Sonata in C minor, op. 10, no. 1, Beethoven).

Both Mozart and Beethoven used aria form with a coda for their slow movements, as, for instance, in Mozart's Andante cantabile from the Sonata in C (K.457). Beethoven has given us many beautiful and moving examples with the long codas which are his special characteristic. Examples known to all are the Largo e mesto from the Sonata in D, op. 10, no. 3, and the great Funeral March from the Sonata in A flat, op. 26.

Those who are interested enough to analyse works for themselves, or have to do so for examination purposes, should keep clearly before their minds the distinct characteristics of sonata form, sonata-rondo, and aria. Sonata form must have a second subject in another key which is at any rate transposed in the recapitulation and nine times out of ten is transposed to the tonic key. This also applies to sonata-rondo, but in this form the principal subject appears again after the second subject and completes the exposition. As some movements in sonata form have new material instead of development in the middle section, and some rondos have development instead of new material, and in the shortened form adopted for slow movements the middle section is sometimes omitted, the above characteristic is the only means of distinguishing the form. In some cases of aria form the first subject appears twice in the first section, as in the Andante from Beethoven's op. 28 in D. But although there is a passage beginning after the first double bar which might be mistaken for a second subject, it is in the tonic key and is not transposed in the reprise. Both Mozart and Beethoven sometimes deck their subjects with such profuse *fiorituri* that a careful scrutiny is required to detect them In the Adagio sostenuto of Beethoven's 'Hammerclavier' Sonata, op. 106, for instance, the recapitulation begins amongst the demisemiquavers commencing three bars after the resumption of the three-sharp key signature.

Variation form has already been discussed in Chapter III. It has been used in each of the four movements of a sonata.

The minuet and trio were derived from the earlier suites. Regarded separately they are in ancient binary form, but regarded as one movement they are in aria form. The trio was so called because it was originally written in only three instrumental parts to give it as much contrast as possible with the minuet which preceded and followed it. The name survived after this custom was abandoned.

Beethoven did not invent the term 'scherzo', for there are humorous movements, some actually called scherzos and others labelled 'scherzando', to be found long before his time. He merely wrote a light-hearted jocular movement instead of the minuet, which was originally stately but even in Haydn's time had often become quite skittish. To begin with, Beethoven's scherzos were of the same length as the minuets and trios and in the same form, but later on he lengthened them out until they reached the proportions of the great culminating scherzo of the Choral Symphony. This is actually in strict sonata form, yet the rhythm, $| \; \rfloor. \; \mathord{\downarrow}\!\!\rfloor \; |$ of the first subject continues throughout. This seems like a contradiction of what was said at the beginning of this chapter about rhythmic contrast. But any monotony is avoided by the exciting pace and character of the movement, and by the longer notes of the second subject, superimposed on the rhythm of the first subject, which at this point becomes merely an accompaniment. The trio is in two-two time and is as full of innocent gaiety as the scherzo is of ferocity.

Beethoven's scherzos contain many different shades of humour, from the fresh girlish laughter of the early scherzos in the Sonatas in A and C, op. 2, nos. 2 and 3, and the gentle fun of the scherzo in the Sonata, op. 27, no. 2, through the more boisterous jokes of the scherzo in the Sonata in D, op. 28, and those of the First, Second, and Third Symphonies, and the more sardonic mood of the one in the Sonata in E flat, op. 31, no. 3 (in two-four time and strict sonata form), to the ferocity of the Choral Symphony.

It will have been noticed that the words 'binary' and 'ternary' have not been used in this chapter except when accompanied by a qualifying term. They are indeed muddling as nomenclature, and give no clue to the actual form, but only to the number of divisions in it.

G

VI

WE now come to the third great change of style in musical history. The first was the revulsion from motet and madrigal at the opening of the seventeenth century to opera and the birth of instrumental music, vocal polyphony having then reached a remarkable state of perfection. The second was the swing over from the counterpoint of the Bach and Handel period to the melody and harmonic colour of Haydn, Mozart, and Beethoven. After Beethoven it was perhaps felt by many composers that he had said all there was to be said in sonata form. At all events it was at this time that the third great change took place with the rise of the romantic movement in Germany. Composers were inspired by stories of valiant knights, distressed damsels, and the like. This outburst of romanticism gave us the wonderful Lieder of Schubert, followed by those of Schumann, Brahms, and Wolf, less wonderful but still beautiful. It also inspired many instrumental compositions. Some of these had romantic titles, like the *Carnaval* and *Davidsbündler* of Schumann. Some were merely called Impromptus, Ballads, or Capriccios, or had some dance rhythm as a foundation like the Waltzes, Mazurkas, and Polonaises of Chopin. But all had the same romantic feeling behind them. Schumann himself said that so long as they conjured up pictures or stories in the imagination of the hearer it mattered not whether these imaginings conformed to the original ideas of the composer.

As these romantic pieces were not on the grand scale of symphony and sonata only a small and simple framework was necessary for them. Hundreds have been written in aria form, many more show their kinship with rondo. Few have much development, and all are easy to follow.

The symphonic tone-poem, being programme music, hardly comes within the scope of this book, for the form is dependent upon the story.

The first thing that strikes us when listening to modern movements on the grand scale—symphonies, chamber music, and sonatas—is that rigid conventions have disappeared, but that all the vital basic principles of form are still there in successful works, and absent in vague and rambling music.

Note-for-note repetition has gone, for it is a throw-back if it appears in the final recapitulation, and causes the music to mark time when isolated sections repeat. A mere restatement is now regarded as waste of time, as it should be. In all repeats new light must be thrown on the themes and new interest stimulated. The other conventions, as for instance the four sections of the exposition, and the dominant key for the second subject, have also disappeared.

But the fundamental ideas, from which all the rules came, have not been lost in the best modern music, for they originated in human nature, which is unchangeable. Love is still the only thing which can cast out fear. When a new departure is due to the fearlessness of love it is good and will stand the test of time. When it springs from the fear of being old-fashioned or plagiaristic, it is a failure. Variety is still the spice of life. Modern experiments which have denuded music of a means of variety and contrast have done harm. Take the matter of tonality. The system of keys has given us two very beautiful means of contrast. New themes are heard on a new key centre. A vague and indefinite tonality can be contrasted with one which is definite. Some modern composers have attempted to write what has been termed 'atonal' music, that is, music without key. But despite its variety and vitality in rhythm and dynamic effects it is monotonous.

We shall find that the modern music which will live has absorbed all the best principles of every period and rejected that which is extreme and revolting.

There must still be an exposition, with themes that can easily be recognized and remembered. It matters not how many there are or in what order we hear them, so long as there are enough to interest us and so long as they are arranged to give contrast and to show each other up to the best advantage.

There must still be a development of themes. The only alternative is new matter, but that leads to vagueness and to padding. There must still be some sort of reprise. No one would like to sacrifice that great moment when the hero returns, nor to forgo the illimitable possibilities which are open to the composer when he prepares our emotions for it.

The subject of harmony does not come within our survey,

but, whilst we are thinking of what is to be discarded and what retained in contemporary music, one cannot help referring to it, for many people are puzzled by certain composers who are eternally searching for means of making music more dissonant. Up to the end of the nineteenth century the discipline was so strict that it tended to repress individuality and cramp expression. There was a natural revolt against all this and it began to be understood that the letter killeth but the spirit giveth life. Like all revolutions this produced extremists, but it enriched harmony and widened its bounds. Harmony—the vertical aspect of music—is only one branch of musical technique and not the most important, for it does not in itself contain movement. Rhythm does, and will always be the dominant factor in musical expression as it is in everything else. What has happened in form has also taken place in harmony: mere conventions have disappeared, but the root principles which gave rise to them, such as the variety to be obtained from the contrast of discord and concord and from the various shades of dissonance, will remain.

In order to appreciate these developments three great symphonic movements will be examined in detail. One is from the transitional period of the nineteenth century and two are from contemporary works: the first movements of Brahms's Fourth Symphony in E minor, the Second Symphony in D of Sibelius, and the London Symphony by Vaughan Williams.

Brahms was fed on the principles of form by his first master, a man named Marxsen. By the time he wrote his first symphony in 1876 at the age of forty-two Brahms was the greatest master of form since Beethoven. In this country it was customary to teach harmony and counterpoint, but the principles and the history of instrumental forms explained in this book, in which Brahms was so thoroughly instructed by Marxsen, were neither taught nor practised. The consequence was that few British musicians were capable of writing extended movements until the period of Stanford and Parry. Even now many students show this weakness in their University exercises. Composition should be taught alongside counterpoint and harmony from the beginning. Brahms's Fourth Symphony was his last. It was first played in 1885. Beethoven's Ninth Symphony was produced in 1824, sixty-one years before Brahms's symphony. But the difference between Beethoven and Brahms is not to be compared with the difference between Brahms and Vaughan Williams, although only thirty-five years elapsed between their works, so greatly has music changed of late.

Brahms had a very orderly mind and a very ingenious brain. Not only was he a master of form but he spent four years working at counterpoint. He was, therefore, peculiarly well equipped as a composer. He was not a melodist of the same fertility or spontaneity as either Mozart or Schubert. He had a romantic nature, but it tended somewhat to the sentimental. He had an instinct for the dramatic and the power to express it, though not to the same extent as Beethoven.

Here is the first subject of his symphony reduced for the piano:

68

You will notice its four distinct sections, all of which are used in the development or the coda later on. It is immediately repeated, this time with a counter-theme thrown from one wood-wind instrument to another. It speaks of heartfelt sadness. After this a martial theme makes its appearance for a moment, and is succeeded by the second theme of the second subject group. (Composers were now writing groups of themes instead of single melodies.) The little tune in B major (Ex. 69) is the only gleam of sunlight in the whole movement:

69

but it is soon held up on a long, gloomy chord (of the diminished seventh) with a string arpeggio running through it and a drum roll beneath it:

70

The clouds have gathered again. The warlike, martial theme reappears pianissimo. It is followed by the gloomy, foreboding chord and arpeggio figure. Now comes the martial theme in full, fortissimo and menacing:

71

This idea of only giving out the beginning of a subject at first, and gradually building it up to its full length at subsequent entries, has since been used by contemporary composers. A cadence in the traditional dominant then concludes the exposition. The older convention was to repeat the exposition. Brahms concedes only a repetition of the first subject, hinted at for eight bars before it arrives. Its former ending is now altered, and the place of its previous repetitions is taken by a new version with the addition of appoggiaturas, thus:

72

This version forms an important part in the development. The gloomy chord, with its upward and downward arpeggio, alternates with the warlike theme. Finally a version of the second part of the first subject, mysterious and sad, sinks into a pianissimo. Then follows a novel recapitulation. It begins with an augmentation of the first four notes of the first subject unaccompanied until the fourth note, when it is harmonized by the gloomy chord. The next four notes are then treated similarly. The composer thus emphasizes and prolongs the pessimistic sadness of the theme. After that the repetition is practically note for note, with the exception of the transposition of the second subject group into the tonic key, until the end of the full statement of the warlike theme. This is succeeded by a tremendous repetition of the first subject in canon between treble and bass. The final cadence (bars 17 to 19 in Ex. 68) is now broadened out to give the impression of finality (seventh bar from the end of the movement), in much the same way as the final cadence in the tune, 'The secret flower', Ex. (49). Truly there is nothing new under the sun!

The next example is the first movement of Sibelius's Second Symphony in D. The first theme simply consists of the third, fourth, and fifth notes of the scale reiterated, accompanied by plain chords over a pedal D. Soon a merry counter-theme appears on top of this figure (Ex. 73 (a)). This is interrupted by repeating its half-cadence, but augmented (Ex. 73 (b)).

73

It then resumes, but is interrupted twice in a similar way before this motive, played by the bassoons, is heard, which leads to a broad string melody (Ex. 74 (a)). This is most effective, for it has character, and stands alone with no supporting harmony.

74

The pause at the eighteenth bar of Ex. 74 is immediately followed by the string figure (Ex. 74 (b)), subsequently to have quite a lot of importance:

74(b)

This is at once succeeded by a wood-wind episode, the first bars of which are given in Ex. 74 (c):

74 (c)

Then follows a pizzicato figure of the same rhythm as the first subject. This leads, with a crescendo and affrettando to the first subject with a loud C sharp held under it and above it by wood-wind and brass. This C sharp has a lively tail which kicks out some quavers.

75

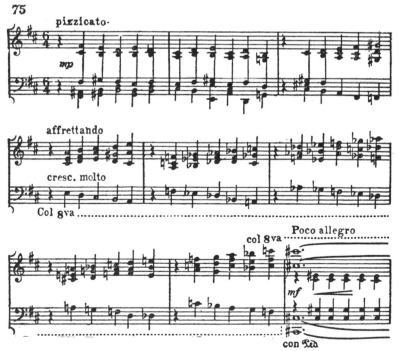

The music has now moved almost imperceptibly to the dominant, or north side, of the original key. There have been no definite perfect cadences; not even dovetailed cadences, as in the Brahms movement, where the new theme begins on the last chord of the previous one. The divisions of the form, although present, are carefully concealed. The constructional support of the building is covered up. A long and exciting crescendo now begins, including a new string figure:

76

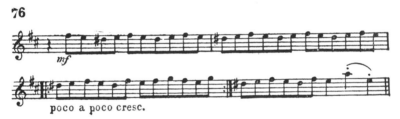

which may have been derived from Ex. 73 (*a*) by diminution and inversion. But all the themes except Ex. 74 (*c*) begin with three notes in scale order, either up or down. This crescendo includes some references to the first subject and leads up to a bold chord of C major, held solidly with no figure beneath it. It turns out, after a bar and a half, to be our friend with the kick in the tail. Partly because a solid chord, especially if it is not an ordinary one which we might expect, succeeding all this exciting movement, makes a startling contrast, and partly because it immediately precedes a phrase in dropping fifths (Ex. 77) which is an important character in this drama, this plain chord of C is *l'expression juste* at the moment when it occurs.

77

Three more references to the first theme, dying away, bring the exposition to a close in the traditional dominant—A. The short themes, all in admirable contrast, yet nearly all subtly related, the pauses which do not seem to pause—the throb of the pulse always seems to go through them, and they all persuade us that something vital will follow them—the economy of notes, all are typical of a great and fearless composer who can bring off things which often spoil the work of lesser men. Mozart and Haydn had to clamour for attention: the modern composer who knows his job and his audience says in music's language, 'Hush! What's this coming?'

The development begins on the oboe with a mysterious version of the long-note-with-kicking-tail theme. Then the bassoon gives an equally mysterious version of the end of the counter-theme (Ex. 73 (b)). This is followed by the dropping fifths (Ex. 77). These two alternate, the strings keeping up the figure given in Ex. 76 as a murmuring background. The keys change rapidly. The short themes, somewhat ordinary on first hearing, begin to bear a deeper significance. Soon we make a new acquaintance with the pizzicato figure given in Ex. 75, now in three bar instead of two bar phrases, played in reiterated notes, and undulating with crescendo and diminuendo. This suddenly evaporates into a tapping on the drum. The clarinet ruminates on the long-note-with-tail: the strings chatter a new version of the first theme with its counter-theme. Along with this the clarinet and bassoon ruminate again, this time on scraps of the episode, the beginning of which is shown in Ex. 74 (c). The music now becomes more exciting on a new development of Ex. 73 (a). A long crescendo finishing with a 'crescendo possible', during which all the themes recur mostly in combination, lands us with a thump on the biggest climax of the movement, for the *dénouement* is not far away now; it is the darkest hour before the dawn. The music therefore approaches the original key. The phrase first played by the bassoon (Ex. 74) is now given to the brass and leads to the second appearance of Ex. 74 (a) thundered out by the brass with an extension made by repeating the eighth bar. This is a new feature— change in the order of the themes in the recapitulation. There is a breath pause, the first tempo is resumed with the counter-theme, Ex. 73 (a), now heard alone. The string figure which accompanies Ex. 74 (c) is now used to bridge over the end of this theme. There is another breath pause and the counter-theme is combined with Ex. 74 (b); thus two themes are recapitulated at the same time. After that things go quite normally with the traditional transposition to the tonic key. There is no coda, and the movement ends in a pianissimo, just as it did at the end of the exposition.

There is no padding in this movement, nor is there any in the Brahms. Both composers give us a plenitude of themes, and then construct the entire movement from them alone. Both have the gift of economy. Brahms makes a long subject and then develops sections of it. Sibelius's themes are short—some, as you have seen, are merely rhythmic figures. But he handles them with consummate skill and invention. He does not despise the old traditions—neither did Brahms—and though he was not afraid to depart from the law when he saw a distinct advantage from it, he always kept the spirit of it.

The first movement of the London Symphony by Vaughan Williams only bears a resemblance to sonata form in that a number of themes are heard, developed, and recapitulated. The movement is not definitely divided by marked cadences into three parts—exposition, development, and reprise—but naturally the beginning is where most of the tunes make their appearance, the middle is where they are developed, and the latter part is where most of the recapitulation takes place.

The slow introduction, with its smooth, gently rising fourths, and its dreamy descending counter-tune:

78

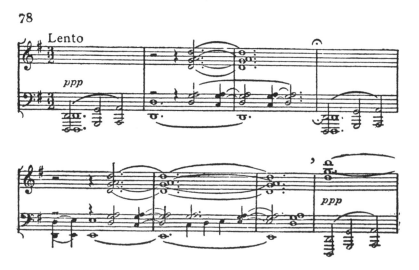

seem to suggest the quiet dawn over the great city. Very soon Big Ben strikes, and then things soon begin to spring to life. The vigorous Allegro commences with a theme in direct contrast—loud instead of soft, quick instead of slow, staccato instead of legato, chromatic instead of diatonic.

79

Observe the rumbling bass at (*a*), for this, in crochet form (Ex. 80), is to be given considerable importance with its variants

80

later on. The two rhythmic cells at (*b*) and a third at (*c*) should also be noted.

The mysteriously quiet mood created at the end of Ex. 79 is maintained for a few bars. The rumble of Ex. 79 (*a*) lies beneath the music, whilst above its crochet form, Ex. 80, in one shape or another provides all the material, until, with a quickening of the pace, another short, rhythmic unit makes its appearance, the rumble still beneath it.

81

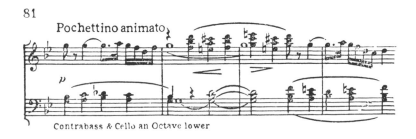

Contrabass & Cello an Octave lower

This is the beginning of the preparation for the entry of one of the main tunes of the movement. During this, two more short rhythmic fragments are heard, which should be duly noted:

82

and 83

a short reference is also made to Ex. 79 (c). There is a diminuendo and a sudden crescendo, then comes the tune, its first two bars blazed forth on wood-wind and brass. It has a real cockney flavour about it, for it is somewhat strident, humorous, and full of vim.

84

H

Ex. 84 really consists of three tunes marked (*a*), (*b*), and (*c*). The second has a distinct folk-song flavour about it: the last has the rhythm of the tango. It is surprising how well they agree in such close proximity. This is the end of the statement of thematic material. Of course there is no full stop; the continuity must not be broken. The boisterous mood is maintained, with a momentary relief when Ex. 84 (*b*) reappears. This is whipped up into a crescendo by reiterating scraps of (*c*) combined with the diminution of the first bar of (*b*). A terrific climax ensues with Ex. 78 thundered out by the bass instruments, leading to a restatement of Ex. 79 with its attendants, (*a*) and (*b*). The music quietens down. We are now in the development section. The rumble of the traffic goes on down below. Above it are heard dreamy reminiscences of Ex. 83 played by the wood-wind. The four notes of the rumble become:

This is the motive for some easy-flowing, close imitation amongst the strings. The flute contributes a little tune derived from the eighth bar of Ex. 84 (*a*):

The bassoon dreamily repeats it. Before it has finished the flute and violins play an augmentation of Ex. 85, whilst the 'cellos and bass clarinet have the normal version. Ex. 81 now reappears: its second and third bars link up with the second bar of Ex. 85 augmented. A double quartet of solo strings and the harp help to increase the ethereal atmosphere. Other short themes—Exx. 82, 83, and 86—float about the orchestra. The counterpoint is comfortable and close-fitting, like a well-made garment. At last this lovely dream is ended and a free recapitulation is commenced with Ex. 79 in the original key, but pianissimo, the rumbling motive accompanying it instead of following it. Even boisterous Ex. 84, when it arrives (much sooner than in the exposition, and transposed to the traditional tonic key), is heard as in a dream. Suddenly the music surges up in a two-bar crescendo to another piece of effective counter-point—the last four bars of Ex. 84 augmented in the higher instruments against the original form in the bass. The music is then lulled into a reprise of the introductory theme (Ex. 78), the counter-tune now coming first and the rising fourths a few bars later, assigned to the wood-wind with a rolling bass figure beneath. One burst of Ex. 84 (c) leads to a coda in which the jolly, devil-may-care, cockney mood is recaught and driven home, Ex. 84 providing most of the material, especially the last four bars.

This great movement bears out what was said on page 99. Here is no formal, note-for-note repetition; each new appear-ance of a theme brings with it fresh treatment and new interest. Nor are the themes repeated in exactly the same order as in the exposition. We can never say for certain what is coming next. If we could we should become *distrait*, just as we should with a novel. All the things worth keeping in the music of our forefathers are to be found here in modern guise: pure melody, masterly counterpoint, the use of key centres, and the art of placing themes so as to show them up by contrast to the best advantage.

From what has been said it will be realized that there is more to listen for in music than the mere sound of it, and that the ability to discover its full content needs a great deal of concentration but is well worth the effort.

No one can express an accurate estimate of music without a knowledge of its history. Readers of this book should now be a little better equipped to do so, for they will have seen how great symphonic movements have grown gradually from the order of cadences in the earliest melodies and from ancient dance forms, and how these forms, originally so conscien-tiously adhered to, have now become foundation principles, the spirit of which remains although the letter is discarded. These principles were founded on human nature, which never changes, and which demands variety and contrast, excitement and tranquillity, and, above all, beauty.

A LIST OF MUSIC ANALYSED, OR REFERRED TO IN THE TEXT

THE following list of music divides itself into three categories. Firstly (List A), works which are referred to many times. These are selected from classics which should be found in every musician's library.

Secondly (List B), works which will materially help in the study of this book, but are not likely to be found in the libraries of the majority of readers. These can often be borrowed either from friends, or from public libraries.

Thirdly (List C), music, chiefly of historical importance, to which only a passing reference is made.

LIST A

BACH: The *Well-tempered Clavier* (the forty-eight Preludes and Fugues). A.E.

BEETHOVEN: The Piano Sonatas. A.E.
The Nine Symphonies. Arranged for piano duet. A.E., or in the form of miniature orchestral scores.

HAYDN: The Piano Sonatas. The Sonata in C, referred to at pages 85 and 86 is to be found in Aug., 8169B.

MOZART: The Piano Sonatas and Variations. A.E.

LIST B

BACH, J. S.: The Organ Works, inlcuding the Choral Preludes. A.E.
The Chaconne for Violin alone. A.E.
The Mass in B minor. A.E.

BACH, C. P. E.: The Clavier Sonatas. Peters, 276.

BRAHMS: Variations on a theme by Handel, opus 24. A.E.
Symphony No. 4 in E minor, opus 98. Min. Sc. Simrock. Gram.

117

BYRD: Prelude in C. *Popular Pieces*, page 3. Aug., 8300A.
Variations on The Carman's Whistle. Ibid., page 21.
Pavan, The Earl of Salisbury. Ibid., page 14.

FRESCOBALDI: Fugue in A minor. Three Fugues for Organ, No. 3. Cramer.

HAYDN: String Quartet in F, opus 77, no. 2. Min. Sc. Gram.

MOZART: Piano Concerto in A (K.488). A.E. Min. Sc. Gram.

PURCELL: Almand in C. *Popular Pieces*, page 23. Aug., 8300E.
Song, 'I attempt from Love's sickness to fly.' *Fifteen Songs and Airs*, Purcell Society's Edition. N.
Song, 'When I am laid in earth,' Dido's Lament, from the Opera, *Dido and Aeneas*. O.U.P., or, singly, *Fifteen Songs and Airs*.

SIBELIUS: Symphony in D, No. 2, opus 43. Min. Sc. Gram.

SWEELINCK: Fantasia in D minor for the Organ. Original Compositions, 402. N.

VAUGHAN WILLIAMS: The London Symphony. Min. Sc., S. & B. Gram.

LIST C

BATTEN: Anthem, 'Deliver us, O Lord.' O.U.P. *Tudor Church Music*, 56.

BUXTEHUDE: Praeludium und Fuge in G minor. *Alte Meister des Organspiels*, page 42. Peters, 4301A.
Praeludium und Fuge in E minor. *Alte Meister*, page 51.

BYRD: Fantasia for strings. *The English Madrigal School*, edited by Fellowes, Vol. xvi, page 166. S. & B.

FROBERGER: Capriccio in G. *Alte Meister* page 94.

GIBBONS: Almaine in C. Orlando Gibbons, *Keyboard Works*, Vol. i, page 8. S. & B.

KERLL: Canzona in C. *Alte Meister*, page 111.

PACHELBEL: Choral Prelude, *Vom Himmel hoch*. *Choralvorspiele Alte Meister*, page 113. Peters, 3048.

SCHEIDT: Choral Prelude, *Vater unser*. *Choralvorspiele Alte Meister*, page 125.

SCHUBERT: Songs. A.E.
 Piano Trio in B flat, opus 99. A.E., Min. Sc. Gram.
TUNDER: Choral Prelude, *Jesus Christus unser Heiland*.
 Choralvorspiele Alte Meister, page 134.
VITALI: Ciaccona for Violin. A.E.

ABBREVIATIONS

A.E.	Any edition.
Aug.	Augener.
Gram.	Gramophone records are obtainable.
Min. Sc.	Miniature Scores are obtainable.
N.	Novello.
O.U.P.	Oxford University Press.
S. & B.	Stainer and Bell.